Griffith

Griffith

First Artist of the Movies

Martin Williams

New York   Oxford
OXFORD UNIVERSITY PRESS
1980

Copyright © 1980 by Martin Williams

Library of Congress Cataloging in Publication Data
Williams, Martin T
  Griffith, first artist of the movies.

  Bibliography: p.
  Includes index.
    1. Griffith, David Wark, 1875-1948.
    2. Moving-picture producers and directors—
  United States—
Biography. I. Title.
PN1998.A3G787   791.43'0233'0924   [B]   79-18609
ISBN 0-19-502685-3

Foreword

My intention has been to offer a critical biography of a remarkable American artist—an account and an interpretation of D. W. Griffith's career and development. I have made no particular effort to uncover new biographical information, but have tried to relate, synthesize, and interpret some of what is already known. Accordingly, when my sources disagreed, I have made my choices—often made them silently—and moved on. (Was it really Lee Dougherty, story editor at Biograph, who first offered Griffith the chance to direct, as Robert M. Henderson says, or was it Henry Marvin, one of the company's founders and its general manager, as others suggest?)

Griffith's Biograph period, as well as the development of his film style, has been dealt with frequently and from several points of view. I have confined my comments on the films largely to indicating major discoveries in cinematic and story-telling techniques, and have tried to treat biographical matters and accounts so that Griffith the man stays prominently in the story. I have also tried to make my description of the films not a substitute, but, I hope, an incentive for seeing even the earliest and simplest of them.

Essential studies of Griffith include Robert M. Henderson's biography, *D. W. Griffith: His Life and Work,* and Edward

Wagenknecht and Antony Slide's anthology, *The Films of D. W. Griffith,* plus Karl Brown's personal and revealing *Adventures with D. W. Griffith.* I hope that my work may be considered a supplement and perhaps a complement to theirs.

My particular concerns have included Griffith's relationship to his father (or, rather, his idea of his father); his view of war and man's individual and collective relationship to it; the nature of Griffith's frustrations at the large studio system which his success virtually created; and the image of the girl-woman through whom he interpreted the world. I have also offered some thoughts on the neglected subject of the relationship of Griffith's film techniques to those of the earlier visual arts—painting and still photography.

I have tried to exercise care and caution in the use of such terms as "popular art" and "popular culture." Having lived with these terms for some years—and having used them myself on occasion—I have become convinced that they often set up misleading expectations and result in a false and sometimes patronizing view of our native artists and our native art forms.

Buster Keaton, although he was enormously popular, may or may not have been a "popular artist," whatever that term may mean when applied to him. But Keaton was even more than a great comedian. He created superb comedic dramas.

And Fred Astaire has been one of the leading dancers of the century, regardless of category or style. Frank Willard, in the original "Moon Mullins," and H. J. Tuthill, in "The Bungle Family," were fine graphic-story satirists. Duke Ellington very likely our greatest composer. And D. W. Griffith the greatest dramatist we have produced.

M. W.

Alexandria, Virginia
March 1980

Acknowledgments

William K. Everson ran films for me from his personal Griffith collection, let me poke around among his books, and generously kept me from making several errors of fact as well. Edward Connor was of considerable help with research. Eileen Bowser let me examine the Griffith papers deposited in the Museum of Modern Art's Department of Film and was otherwise encouraging. Also, I was guided through the film collection at the Library of Congress by Barbara Humphrys.

I am most grateful to them all.

Contents

Illustrations

All illustrations, except on page 103, are used through the courtesy of The Museum of Modern Art/Film Stills Archive.

Griffith

One

Magic
in a Schoolroom

One evening in the 1870s, a small boy sat beside his father in a darkened classroom of a Kentucky village schoolhouse, entranced at the sight of a magic-lantern show. The lantern, something like a modern slide projector, offered pictures of wonderful, far-away places and it told stories. The stories were told sometimes with exotic drawings and sometimes with photographed scenes of posed actors or models, and there was a narrator standing beside the screen describing the action. It is appropriate that one of the earliest memories of David Wark Griffith should have been of that magic-lantern show, for, in not too many years, the magic of the lantern projector would have been replaced for most people by the magic of the moving picture. By 1908, Griffith himself was involved with the motion picture as a director. And within a few years, he had become its greatest artist—its first true artist according to most film historians.

Terry Ramsaye, in what is still one of the most reliable histories of the early movies in the United States, *A Million and One Nights,* said that Griffith "in 1908 . . . began to assemble the mechanical and optical properties of the motion picture into a new dramatic technique peculiar to the screen." Within four years, declared Iris Barry, curator of the Film Library of the Museum of Modern Art,

Griffith laid down all the basic principles of the medium. Director
Cecil B. De Mille said, "Griffith had no rivals. He was the teacher
of us all." And director Rex Ingram once admitted. "He did everything first. . . . All that the best of us can do is watch what D. W.
does next and imitate as best we can." The great comedian, Charlie
Chaplin, indicating that it was not only an art that Griffith had
founded, added that "the whole industry owes its existence to him."

It is also significant that Griffith should have remembered it was
his father who took him to the magic-lantern show. Like many another of Griffith's memories involving his father, however, the story
may or may not have been true. As Griffith told it later, the family
farm in Kentucky, near the community of Crestwood in Oldham
County, had been built up by his father, Jacob Griffith. But in the
early days of the Civil War, the Union Army had burned it down,
and its fields lay largely unused and overgrown with weeds until
the war ended. When Jacob Griffith had returned home from his
service as a colonel in the Confederate Army, as his son later told
it, he built a small farmhouse on his land and attempted to return
to his life as a gentleman farmer. But he and his family did not
prosper in the poverty of the post-Civil-War South. His health was
not good. And Jacob Griffith was a somewhat improvident man.

David was born in the farmhouse on January 23, 1875, and he
knew his father for only the first seven years of his life, for the elder
Griffith died in 1882. "I think the one person I really loved most in
all my life," Griffith said in later years, "was my father. I often
wondered if he cared anything about me particularly. I am forced to
doubt it. As far as I can remember, he never seemed to show to
anybody his feelings toward them. But he must have had a deep
emotional nature behind his sternness. What he did, which he did
only occasionally, was to put his hand on my head and say, 'Son,
how are you this day?' This simple action seemed an overwhelming
miracle of some kind."

The boy learned that his forebears had come to America from
Wales before the Revolution. His great-grandfather had fought in

that war and afterward had settled in Virginia as a planter. Young David also heard from his father about other and more fabled ancestors. "You are descended from Kings. David, the Apt-Griffith, King of Wales." And he learned that the Latin words on the Griffith family coat of arms, *virtus omnia nobilitat,* meant "virtue ennobles everything."

Jacob Griffith, David's father, had been a wanderer and a loner as a young man. He left Virginia while still in his teens, and went to Kentucky where he studied medicine and briefly practiced it in the town of Floydsburg. Before long, however, he had given up medicine and was fighting in the Mexican War under General Zachary Taylor. Afterward, he returned to Kentucky and married Mary Oglesby. In 1850, he left his wife and three children to go west as the escort for a wagon train from Missouri to California during the last days of the Gold Rush. He returned home to his farm after that trip and, in 1853-54, served as a member of the Kentucky legislature.

When the Civil War broke out, Jacob Griffith became a colonel under General "Stonewall" Jackson. He suffered five wounds, one of which was so severe that he was left for dead on the battlefield. Only his moans, overheard by a doctor, saved him. This physician sewed up his abdomen while the Colonel bit down on the brim of his hat to keep from crying out. The only available surgeon's catgut was of an inferior grade, and it was from the effects of this makeshift operation that Colonel Griffith eventually died. At another point during the war's action, Jacob Griffith, so badly wounded in his shoulder and leg that he was unable to walk or ride a horse, led a victorious cavalry charge from a buggy.

From his father, then, David learned of the heroism and horror of war. The elder Griffith was a natural storyteller, and he beguiled his children also with tales of his adventures in Texas and the West. From his father, too, David got his first glimpses of the theatrical arts, even before the magic-lantern show. Jacob Griffith had a particularly strong and resonant voice. It was loud enough that he had acquired nicknames like "Roarin' Jack" and "Thunder Jake" on the battlefield. And it was expressive enough that his Sunday evening recitations and readings from the Bible and Shakespeare were celebrated events in and around Crestwood. David was not required to attend these events, but he always did, even before he could understand the meaning of his father's words.

Thus, David Griffith grew up in genteel poverty, in an atmosphere of high traditions and former glories, of courtly and gracious manners, and of very real and perceptible straits. Or that, at any rate, was the image of his father and his boyhood that D. W. Griffith offered to others, particularly in the years of his fame. Many Southern families impoverished after the Civil War offered similar stories of former glory, noble heritage, and more genteel times. But for many a Southern family the truth was somewhat different. And so it was with the Griffiths.

Griffith's grandfather had not been a captain in the War of 1812, as was claimed, but a private with one month's undistinguished service. Jacob Griffith, as Robert Henderson reveals, was without a trade until he talked a local doctor in Floydsburg, Kentucky (John Speers, a man of somewhat dubious training himself), into an apprenticeship of only two years' duration. And Jacob himself proved a failure at the profession. In mid-1846, Jacob Griffith enlisted in the Kentucky Cavalry, where his roaring voice on the drill fields gained him promotion to sergeant before he joined forces with Zachary Taylor in the Mexican War. At the end of a year, however, he failed to re-enlist and left the service in New Orleans, returning soon to Floydsburg as a self-proclaimed hero and marksman—and a physician with very few patients. He married Mary Oglesby, whose father Thomas built the couple a cottage on the 495-acre family farm, which Jacob was of course expected to help operate. However, Jacob's status quickly became more like that of a hired hand—and apparently a not very reliable one. In 1850, Jacob Griffith left with two of his wife's brothers and his former mentor Dr. Speer for the recently discovered gold fields of California, but with little ultimate success.

The elder Griffith was home again in two years; he had quite early lost his leadership of the group by his bad temper, and whatever money he had brought with him (which may have belonged to his wife's uncle and not to him) in a card game. He became again a physician without patients, a part-time farm-worker, a dramatic orator on the California gold fields at church socials, and (in a logical step) a politician who got himself elected to the state legislature in Louisville. Eventually, he also inherited half of his father-in-law's farm through his wife. The secession of Kentucky from the Union in 1861 gave Jacob Griffith a chance to escape the drudgery (and failure) of farm management and to rejoin the military, where he did rise to the rank of colonel, although he probably did not lead any cavalry charge from a buggy.

After the War, Jacob Griffith returned to the farm which his wife had managed splendidly in his absence. It had never been threatened by the Union Army, and former slaves had remained as employees, tenant farmers, with a small annual salary. Jacob Griffith sat on the farmhouse porch; drank; beguiled his children with stories of a romantic past and a brave and noble War Between the States; from time to time returned briefly to Kentucky politics; read aloud from Poe, Scott, and Shakespeare; and drank. By March 1882, he was dead.

D. W. Griffith remembered his mother as also dedicated to an aristocratic concept of family pride. "Always remember who you are," she told him. She would never allow him to be called Davey either. His name, she explained, meant Dearly Beloved, beloved of God. Griffith later said that he saw the face of Jesus in the icicles that had formed on the branches of a tree as he walked to school on a winter morning. He spoke to it. He told his vision that he hoped that Jesus liked him a little because he, David, loved Him and always would.

Griffith also had many special memories from his youth of his sister Mattie who was something of a surrogate mother to him. It was she who sat with him on the front stoop just before bed time and tried to answer all the boy's questions about the skies, the stars, and the wonders of the world. She, as well as his father, had tutored David in reading even before he began to attend the village school.

The beauties and hardships and details of the countryside, of farm life, and of small town life that he had known as a child stayed with Griffith all his life, and showed up in his films. Griffith remembered a beloved yellow dog who minded the small flock of sheep on the Griffith place. One day, as such dogs sometimes will, this dog turned on one of the sheep and mauled it. David knew that it meant the dog would have to be shot, and he behaved bravely when his father took it out in the field to end its life. He did not later turn the incident into a Biograph film, but he might have. In his later years, Griffith also remembered how he would play alone in the abandoned old "big" house on the property of his mother's family. Surely he imagined a former life in this place as his father had described it to him.

There were seven Griffith children, but David often played alone. He did some of the farm work, too, of course, and would drive the cows home from pasture to the barn as dusk fell when he was still quite small. One day, he fended off a bully who threatened to beat him up during his walk to school. More possible vignettes for future films.

After the Colonel's death, his widow discovered that Jacob Griffith had negotiated several mortgages on the property and was paying 10 per cent compound interest on them. Clearly, the farm could no longer pay the way for the large family. But they knew farming, and Mrs. Griffith was able to move them to another and a smaller farm. The experiment did not last long, however, and it was soon evident that the smaller farm could not support them. At Mattie's urging, Mary Griffith found a rooming and boarding house in Louisville which she could run. It was in a poor neighborhood to be sure, and it was not the kind of life that she had been used to, but there would be space for the children, food for the table, and work for them all that would perhaps not be so back-breaking. They would make out. And so they piled the few possessions they had left onto a two-horse wagon and headed for the city. David rode on top, his head full of anticipation. There would be no more heavy work in the tobacco field. No driving the cows home at dusk. There would be no more struggles with the heavy horse-drawn plow. No more small farm chores. "We are going to live in the city!," he remembered thinking excitedly. "Hooray!"

The Griffiths' wagon rode through the center of Louisville. And there was Griffith sitting stiffly on top of the heap of belongings, his hair needing cutting, his jeans too short for his thin legs and inches above the tops of his heavy rawhide shoes. And there was a pair of wide red suspenders much in evidence across his chest and back. The first greetings given this family of obvious "Country Jakes" by the city folks were far from cordial. The country was then in the period now called the Gay Nineties and, despite the long-lingering poverty that followed on the Civil War and the social upheavals of "Reconstruction" that followed it, Louisville seemed an active city to the young man. There were shops that sold just about anything one could think of. There were restaurants and cabarets. The streets were full of colorful people from up and down the great rivers of the Middle West. The Mississippi meets the Ohio River in Kentucky, and Louisville is on the Ohio. There were salesmen, gamblers, beautiful women. There were musicians, some of whom even played a new kind of Afro-American syncopated music soon to become ragtime.

There were actors, too. Theater was an important part of social and intellectual life in American cities then, and Louisville had several theaters. There was an auditorium, where really big attractions like the band of the March King, John Philip Sousa, might appear; or where Sarah Bernhardt, the world-celebrated French actress, would perform on one of her American tours. In the Avenue Theatre, one could see lurid melodrama with an emphasis on horror and blood. There was a Masonic Temple Theatre where audiences supported a variety of plays performed by a company of local actors. At the Buckingham, there was low comic lampoon. The Bijou had variety (or vaudeville, as it soon came to be known). Macauley's Theatre became nationally famous, for here was produced the first play ever done in the United States by Henrik Ibsen, the great Norwegian dramatist, and here appeared celebrated actors from all over the world. And there was Beirod's Concert Hall with its musical performances of classics and light classics.

It was immediately required that the schoolboy David also work to help out the family. He was a cash boy (a sort of apprentice cashier) in Lewis' Dry Goods Store for a while, and he did not like running into prosperous customers who knew him and had known his father. He worked in the offices of *The Louisville Courier*. He ran an elevator for another dry goods retailer; his piping voice, calling out the floors, "carpets, rugs, draperies, curtains," became familiar to the customers. But the most interesting job for the young man was undoubtedly when he helped out at the bookshop of the Flexner brothers. The bookstore was run by Bernard and Washington Flexner, of a remarkable family of Jewish intellectuals. Their brother Simon Flexner later became head of research for the Rockefeller Foundation; sister Mary wrote plays; Lincoln Flexner was a school principal; Jacob a physician; and Abraham owned the Flexner School. The shop was a gathering place for local writers, including Mary Johnson, James Whitcomb Riley, and Eugene Field. David loved the place. But he did not work so hard at his job as he did at reading the store's books, and he often heard the gentle voice of Bernard or Washington Flexner saying, "David, don't you think it would be better if you spent less time in reading books and more time in trying to sell them? A little more attention to the customers, and perhaps if the shelves and books were dusted more frequently. . . ."

Because he was still young and because he was poor, Griffith necessarily stood aside from the life of Louisville, with its fashionable restaurants and clubs. Attending the theater was a hardship to him, but he did not stay away altogether. And considering the romantic glimpses of theater his father had given him, he probably could not have stayed away. One of the first plays he saw was a French melodrama called *The Two Orphans* starring Kate Claxton, a theater piece he would return to in later life. And one evening, from a high gallery, second balcony seat, which had cost only ten cents. he saw the celebrated Julia Marlowe in *Romeo and Juliet*. He was deeply moved. He determined to become a playwright, an American Shakespeare. Griffith was also taking singing lessons, and he got not only valuable voice training but an acquaintance with opera and with the more colloquial "popular" music, which his teacher Annie Baustead actually preferred.

David Griffith was into his adolescence. He was gaining height, but he was still thin and loose jointed, and had the strong "beak" nose that so characterized his distinguished face in manhood. He began writing. He regularly visited the library, where he fell into conversation with a young man of his own age named Edmund Rucker. Edmund found David hard to get to know at first, but he noticed that he had a vocabulary with a lot of big words and anyone could tell he had read a lot. Griffith had taken an interest in local history and he outlined a plot for a play based on the local tradition that, when the Duke of Orleans was exiled in the aftermath of the French Revolution, he had come to Kentucky and settled on the Ohio River. David's story had the Duke falling in love with a beautiful Kentucky lady, but eventually renouncing his love to return to his homeland and his duty to become King Louis Philippe. Excited by the story, David and Edmund found many hours to explore the edge of the river, searching for the cabin in America that the Duke was supposed to have lived in.

When he was about eighteen, Griffith spent a summer on the farm of his older brother Will at La Grange to help out with the work. But he spent more time with the local children in a big storage room reciting Shakespeare for them, and flourishing his father's Civil War sword. Thus did the son imitate, and perhaps justify, the father.

In Max Davidson, an aspiring Louisville actor, he met a young man who had once worked professionally and was therefore something of a guide and mentor to theater circles and theatrical traditions. Davidson, of German-Jewish heritage, also told him of the "Freedom Hall" on Market Street, where radical ideas like Populism, trade unionism, and socialism were discussed. Griffith was not unsympathetic, but neither was he deeply impressed.

Griffith got on stage once, too, as a "super" (supernumerary or, in movie parlance, "extra") with one of the huge touring productions at the Auditorium. Such companies would hire local people in each city to fill out the stage in crowd scenes. David Griffith became convinced that the way to learn stagecraft was to work in the theater, preferably as an actor. But he remained convinced that playwrighting should be his career. When he made his intentions known to his mother, she was horrified that he should take up this still disreputable profession, particularly a young gentleman of Griffith's supposed background and heritage. It would be sinking too low, his mother felt. But David was determined. He took the name of "Lawrence" Griffith in deference to his family's feelings and sought work on stage.

A local man, a Louisville riverboat blacksmith named Ellis, organized a troupe of amateurs and somehow set up a tour of nearby small towns. Their director was one Edward Risley, who claimed experience on the riverboats doing blackface comedy. They were not good, but Griffith later said that they did manage to escape their heckling audiences alive. The blacksmith, often unable to pay for housing his troupe, hit upon the scheme of offering stage experience and a part ownership of the troupe to his various landlords. The troupe ended up with more landlords than actors or managers.

When Griffith returned to Louisville from this disaster, he managed to get an audition with the Merfett Stock Company, which was appearing at the Masonic Temple Theatre. The twenty-two-year-old Lawrence Griffith was an imposing presence on stage: tall, lean, handsome, with a compelling voice that rang clearly to the last row of the gallery. He got the job. But, Griffith later said, the

Merfett Company manager confessed to him afterward that he felt him "too grand" for their troupe. Perhaps he meant too hammy.

Griffith did supporting roles at the Temple for the rest of the Louisville season of 1897-98, and returned briefly for the end of the 1898-99 season. Meanwhile, he toured nearby with Merfett. He played a footman in *Little Lord Fauntleroy,* Parker Serrant in *Lady Windermere's Fan,* and Athos in *The Three Guardsmen.* He had become an actor.

Two

An Actor, a Writer, and a Girl

The way of "Lawrence" Griffith, actor, was not easy. Theater was a major form of entertainment at the time, but there were many actors. And work for most of them was scarce and highly irregular. Pleasing the public was a necessity, and it was never an easy task. Knowing in advance whether something—perhaps something innovative—will please the public was, and is, more difficult still. Even the best actors in a promising play, on a tour that looked good on paper, might find themselves stranded, without audiences or income, far from the big centers where the next part might be found and the next play cast and rehearsed. So, besides acting, Griffith found himself working in a steel mill. He signed aboard a ship that carried lumber along the West Coast. Once, with no money and no prospects of work, he rode a freight train across country, begged for his meals, and finally arrived back in Louisville on foot, his shoes tied with rags, bitterly cold and hungry. He endured such failures. In later years, he said they had made him strong in body, and he knew they had shown him a variety of men and conditions under which they lived, and these experiences became invaluable to him.

In 1905 Griffith was in San Francisco. He had arrived there after a successful year's tour with a well-known leading lady, Ada

D. W. Griffith: a favorite portrait.

Gray, and after a run in Chicago with the Neill Alhambra Stock
Company, during which Griffith appeared as Abraham Lincoln.
A young actress named Linda Arvidson remembered about the
Alhambra Company:

> I was to appear as a boy servant in "Fedora." I remember only
> one scene. It was in a sort of court room with a civil officer sitting
> high and mighty and calm and unperturbed behind a high desk. I
> entered the room and timidly approached the desk. A deep stern
> voice that seemed to rise from some dark depths shouted at me, "At
> what hour did your master leave *Blu Bla?"*
>
> I shivered and shook and finally stammered out the answer,
> and was mighty glad when the scene was over.
>
> Heavens! Who was this person anyhow?

She found out of course. Lawrence Griffith was really David Wark
Griffith, and he did not intend to reveal his real name until he had
made his mark in the world. Griffith, the loner, the quiet man, was
attracted to this intelligent young actress and before long was telling her a bit about his aspirations. As she listened to him, it seemed
to her that he would make his mark. Still, he seemed a bit imprac-
tical and lackadaisical about it all, and she wondered if he would
make it as an actor, or a stage director, or an opera star, a poet,
a playwright, or a novelist—they all seemed real possibilities for
him. Perhaps what Griffith actually conveyed was what many a
self-described Southern aristocrat has conveyed—that all would come
because the world owed it to him, after all.

Griffith told the young actress authoritatively that she should
never get married if she was serious about a stage career. He told
her about the theatrical centers in other parts of the country, in
New York particularly, and he seemed convinced that she would
succeed there on the basis of her "wonderful eyes." She invited him
to lunch at her place and he opened up about his own boyhood,
about his father, and about the South. As he revealed it, it seemed
to her to be a romantic world indeed. Griffith, on his part, knew

that it was rare that a young woman should be attracted to him—
it did not happen to him often. And Linda Arvidson's obvious interest pleased and flattered him.

Fedora was one of three plays in a repertory season with an actor named Melbourne MacDowell as leading man. When it had run its course in the Bay City, Griffith was able to find some brief jobs with local companies. To save money, he managed to move into a single room with the MacDowell company's stage carpenter.

He was still seeing Miss Arvidson, and he continued his writing on the side. Sometimes he combined both activities, dictating to her as they enjoyed an outing to Ocean Beach if a fogless day presented itself. She learned that he had a trunk full of manuscripts—plays long and short, stories, poems. It seemed to her unsophisticated soul that the world was cruel indeed not to appreciate such a genius. One day he showed her a playlet of his called *In Washington's Time* and revealed that it had once been done as a part of a vaudeville bill on the Keith circuit of vaudeville theaters. Perhaps the world was not entirely insensitive to his talents.

Griffith did not seem to worry, even at the gloomiest prospects and even with the flattest purse. It was approaching the season for hop picking in the northern California fields. In those days, field work was not the exclusive province of migrant workers; all sorts of men, women, and children might join in a harvesting for extra money—even for the fun of it. The harvesters could live a rather camp-like existence in the open during this dry season, work by day, and dance and sing and perhaps drink "dago red" wine before sleep at night. Griffith joined them near Ukia. He was impressed with the plain, thrifty people he met there, particularly the newly settling Italians, who sang arias from operas that Griffith knew too. The sextet from *Lucia* was then a field favorite as they worked. And Griffith did not forget to send a box of the sweet-smelling hops back to Linda.

Back in San Francisco, Griffith sold his playlet, *In Washington's Time*, to the Orpheum Theatre on a variety bill, with himself

Young "Lawrence" Griffith on stage. The play was called "Miss Petticoats."

and Linda performing. A projected tour of the play did not materialize, however, and Linda Arvidson took a theatrical job in Los Angeles, while he found brief theater work in San Francisco. Then David heard about a production of *Ramona* that was headed for southern California. The play was a popular romance about American Indians that tried to tell something of their side of the story, and Griffith had played in it before. He got the job, and was able to rejoin Linda in Los Angeles. It was a first, brief acquaintance with a city that was to be important in his later life.

So it went. A job here. A job there. Then in the spring of 1906, there came an offer which would take Griffith back East. It wasn't much, doing bit parts and understudying in the company of the popular actress Nance O'Neill, but it would take him eventually to New York. And it worked out well. One evening he took over the role of the Pastor in a play called *Magda* for an actor who was ill, and he did so well that Miss O'Neill began to give him larger roles for the rest of the tour. Incidentally, one of the plays in Miss O'Neill's repertory was *Judith of Bethulia,* a work based on the Biblical Apocrypha.

Linda Arvidson was on Griffith's mind during that tour. His company was in Milwaukee on April 18th, when news reached him and the rest of the world of a terrible earthquake in San Francisco that had destroyed parts of the city. Linda was able to telegraph David that she was more or less all right, although her money, clothes, and possessions had been lost in the disaster and fire that followed. Her telegram was delayed, however, and delivered to Griffith only by mail. A week later, she had a letter from him inviting her to join him in Boston where the company was booked for six weeks. Donning ill-fitting, hand-me-down clothes that had been distributed by the Red Cross, Linda Arvidson took her place in a line of people on Filmore Street where free railroad tickets were being distributed to the worst victims of the earthquake.

"Where to?" said the man when she finally reached the desk.

"Boston."

"What is your occupation?"

"Actress."

With no further questions, he handed her a complex ticket, nearly a yard long. And on May 9th, she was on board a train that left Oakland, in her lap a lunch of fried chicken provided by helpful neighbors. To most of those who knew him in later life, it seemed strange that D. W. Griffith had ever married at all. It seemed to them that he had always been married only to his work and his great discoveries about the craft and the art of storytelling on film. But, in a way, it was his marriage, and the added responsibilities it gave him, that led him to the movies in the first place.

When Linda Arvidson arrived at the station in Boston and looked out of the train window, she saw a city that seemed impossibly abustle with people who neither knew nor cared about the terrible things that had happened to her out West, nor the important things that were about to happen to her in the East. Then, faster than it takes to tell it, there was her husband-to-be and they were in a taxi. He revealed a license (but of course no ring—that would have cost too much), and they were to be married at the Old North Church—yes, the church where Paul Revere had hung the signal lantern for "one if by land."

In late June of 1906, the couple arrived at their true destination, New York City, in the middle of a heavy thunderstorm which rather frightened the bride. Theatrical activity was fairly slow for the summer, but they sublet a furnished apartment on West 56th Street, which in those days overlooked the open air athletic grounds of the Y.M.C.A., and they started to line up work for the following fall. They managed to do so surprisingly soon. The Reverend Thomas Dixon, a minister-turned-writer, had had considerable success with a novel and play about the post-Civil-War South called *The Clansman*. He was now putting together a tour for another play to be called *The One Woman*. Griffith secured the lead and his wife was made one of the understudies. But that was for the fall. Meanwhile, there was the rest of the summer and the problem of eating. Griffith did day jobs. He could earn $2.25 a day scraping rust from the supports in the new New York subway. True, for his pride's sake, he would leave his apartment building with his overalls concealed, and put them on over his clothes in the first available alley.

Both he and his wife were good at cooking and could do very well by inexpensive groceries. He would work at the stove while singing a favorite Italian aria or a Southern Negro song. And in a true manifestation of the American dream, he might awaken in the morning saying aloud, "I wonder if that meat dish could be canned!" referring to his concoction of the previous evening. More often, however, he might say something like, "I hate to see her die in the third act!" For Griffith's main occupation during these summer months was writing. His chief project was a play to be called *A Fool and a Girl,* based on his experiences on the West Coast and including an act laid in the hop fields. He also used some of the Mexican melodies he had taught to actors in *Ramona.* Another act was set in the Poodle Dog, a San Francisco café. Linda typed the play from his dictation on a second-hand typewriter she had picked up on Amsterdam Avenue.

When the Dixon play opened in Norfolk, Virginia, Griffith was getting $75 a week and his wife $35. After a month's run, however, another actor offered to play the lead at half Griffith's salary and Dixon accepted. The couple went back to New York very nearly without money. Griffith did get a small part in a production of *Salome,* but it didn't last long and he went back to trying to sell *A Fool and a Girl.*

On Christmas Eve 1907, Linda Griffith was preparing a far-from-festive meal of hamburgers, potatoes, a small five-cent pie, and a pint bottle of beer, which she cooled on the window ledge. When D. W. came home and they sat down to eat, she saw that the plates were upside down—had she set them that way and forgotten? What was this anyway? As she turned hers over, she noticed a funny look on her husband's face. There was a slip of paper under the plate. A rent receipt? No, a check for $700 payable to David W. Griffith. He had sold *A Fool and a Girl* through contacts made during the run of *Salome.* It was to be the vehicle for a return to the stage by the then celebrated actress Fannie Ward. There was no question now of leaving New York for a theatrical job, they concluded; they had to be there when rehearsals started for the play. And they had some money to tide them over, too. Then in quick succession Griffith sold a poem to *Leslie's Weekly* magazine for $6 and a short story to *Cosmopolitan* for $75. He was encouraged about his writing—a play, a poem, and a story had sold.

Soon money was running low again. Griffith got an offer to go to Norfolk, Virginia, in a show called *Pocahontas.* It was to be for six weeks, not long enough to conflict with the rehearsals for *A Fool and a Girl,* so he took it. But it lasted only three weeks, and the actors did not receive full pay even for those. However, there was still his own play coming up. *A Fool and a Girl* opened in Washington, D.C., and the couple managed to get just enough cash together to attend. It lasted one week, and then moved to Baltimore for one week. Then it closed. That was that. And the Griffiths rode back to New York in misery.

Somehow, they managed to survive the winter. As Linda later remembered it, a San Francisco bank confirmed that a few hundred dollars in her name had survived the quake. That bit of luck restored Griffith's enterprising zest and optimism. He went to work on a play about the American Revolution to be called *War,* and he approached his subject in a way that was new to him. He and Linda spent hours in the Astor Library, near Eighth Street and Third Avenue, poring over the historical records and paying particular care to copying out passages from the diaries and letters of soldiers involved in the conflict.

The Griffiths managed to entertain a bit in their pursuit of the literary life. They invited Perriton Maxwell, editor of *Cosmopolitan,* to dinner, and Linda Griffith carefully marked the shabby furniture in their two-room flat with small signs, precautionary jokes with serious undertones: "Do not sit there. The springs are weak" was pinned to the sofa. "Don't lean; the legs are loose" was posted on a table. Before the salad was served, supplies were so depleted that Linda rushed out to a nearby pawnbroker to exchange a gold bracelet for the money to get more.

Griffith, in his early thirties, with the responsibilities of a marriage, had discovered that the life of a writer was as full of disappointment and anguish as that of an actor. He admitted that at least so far he had been a failure as a performer and man of the theater, as a playwright, a poet, a short-story writer. Yet his interest and ambition clung to all these things. Something was about to happen to him that would combine these talents, and others, in a way that would be new to the world, and in a way that would bring him very close to fulfilling his youthful, naïve dream of becoming an American Shakespeare.

Three

Encounter
with the Kinetoscope

Winter passed somehow, and spring of 1908 arrived. D. W. Griffith continued to spend his days and his evenings pursuing the work he knew. He made the rounds of producers' offices for work in the theater. And he wrote.

It happened that one day, during a particularly discouraging series of rounds, Griffith ran into an old friend whom he had not seen since Louisville, Max Davidson. Each man told the other briefly all that had happened to him during the past ten years, no doubt stressing successes over failures, and fat times over lean. But then Griffith indicated that the recent months hadn't exactly been a triumph for him, that he had been, as actors put it, "resting between jobs."

How about the motion pictures, Davidson wanted to know. Had he tried them? Griffith didn't know much about the movies. He'd heard of them but wasn't sure he'd actually seen any—not any that used real actors, anyway. He didn't know they did. Movies had been something of a lifesaver to him, Davidson admitted. There was the Biograph outfit down on Fourteenth Street. Up in the Bronx, there was the Edison studio. Over in the wilds of Brooklyn, there was Vitagraph. There were others, too, Davidson continued. Lubin in

Philadelphia, and film companies in Chicago and Los Angeles. New ones were springing up every day. The work is easy, Davidson explained. Films pay three dollars for a day's work—five if you played a lead. Just see Mr. McCutcheon down at Biograph. Griffith's first thought, like that of so many actors at the time, went something like this: "But suppose some of my friends saw me in one of these films! I'd be finished as an actor." Well, Davidson could tell him this: they were very happy to get real actors, treated them special. As a matter of fact, Mr. McCutcheon down at Biograph might even arrange for actors to get off by eleven in the morning if they had an appointment with a theater man.

It is not surprising that Griffith as an actor and writer knew little about the movies in 1908, and that he looked down on them, although the invention, pictures that move, or seem to move, had been around for some time. The public had first been attracted to the idea when little machines called Edison Kinetoscopes had appeared in "penny arcades." The customer dropped a coin in a slot and peeped through a viewer to see a picture that moved. Actually, he was seeing a series of still pictures printed on cards that flipped rapidly by. There were no plots, just people or things in some kind of movement—a man sneezed vigorously, a woman got kissed on the cheek (that one created a minor scandal at the time), a lady named Annabelle did her "butterfly dance." Since about 1890, it had been possible to print images on a strip of transparent film and project them onto a large screen before an audience. So by 1896, it had become common to see moving images projected on screens, in certain vaudeville houses in big cities, as a kind of novelty at the end of a program. The subjects frequently were photographed vaudeville acts.

In 1901, however, American vaudeville performers struck against the theaters in vast numbers for higher pay, and films found themselves all over the vaudeville bills, and sometimes the only thing on the bills. Projection equipment, therefore, was manufactured in quantity and installed widely. Inevitably, the strike of live variety performers ended, and with it the demand for projectors. Manufacturers were overstocked and cut their prices. Many theater-owners were now willing to sell off their machines at second-hand. With such equipment available cheap, there sprang up a new kind of theater that came to be called the "nickelodeon." A small entrepreneur, perhaps the same man who had at first put Kinetoscopes into his "penny arcade," rented an empty store, installed a projector and a screen, rented or bought some films, got some chairs, charged a five-cent admission, and found himself enjoying a phenomenal success.

By 1908 there were about 10,000 of these little theaters across the country. They stayed open about twelve hours of the day in the big cities, and showed a program of brief subjects that lasted about a half an hour. There were actions like those the Kinetoscope had offered, or vaudeville turns, or thrilling shots like that of a train headed straight for the camera, or brief incidents and anecdotes, some of them comic (two naughty boys sic a dog on a woman carrying a basket of clothes on her head; a pompous, overdressed gentleman falls down the steps of a front stoop and crushes his silk hat). Before long there were simple little stories. There were commercials, too—slides were shown of ads for local merchants. Other slides might advise, "Ladies will please remove their hats" or "No Smoking or Spitting Allowed." "Nice" people did not consider these little places of entertainment respectable, and "real" actors felt these "galloping tintypes," as they called them, were beneath them. Well, not *all* "real" actors.

Our account above of Griffith's encounter with Max Davidson comes from Linda Arvidson Griffith. D. W. himself was perhaps remembering the same incident when years later he told of running into Harry Salter, not Davidson, having a cup of coffee in a place with the marvelous name of Three-Cent John's Eating Emporium. He seated himself across the table from Salter, an acting acquaintance whose doleful expression had earned him the name of "Gloomy Gus." Naturally the two fell into conversation about prospects, and Salter suggested films to Griffith, specifically the Edison Company and a man named Edwin S. Porter. "Besides," Salter added, "he's always looking for stories for his motion pictures. And you're a writer." Griffith said something about not having sunk so low as to try the movies. Salter replied with a gloomy shrug that it was better than not eating.

Salter had planted an important idea. When Griffith reported the conversation to Linda that evening, she too was reluctant that they try the movies as a medium for their acting talents. But for David as a writer, well, perhaps that was different. So with Griffith dictating to her typewriter, they wrote up a synopsis of the popular Puccini opera *La Tosca*. The following morning, Griffith rode the Third Avenue "El" up to the Bronx to the studios of the Edison Motion Picture Company. Edison's was an unusual building; all windows and skylights, it seemed to be made of glass—the better to let in the sunlight for photography. He found director Edwin S. Porter easily and presented him with his outline. Porter looked it over and decided it had too many scenes, and was maybe a little pretentious for a film anyway. At this point, Griffith in his disappointment made a quick decision that went directly against his previous thinking. He admitted he was an actor, too. After all, "Lawrence" Griffith the actor wasn't exactly D. W. Griffith the writer. Anyway, in those days, neither writers nor actors were given credit in the titles of the films themselves.

"Well, I am looking for a man for a part," said Porter, sizing up the fellow standing before him. "But it is a sort of woodsman-mountaineer part and I don't think you are husky enough for it."

"I could pad up for it a bit," said Griffith.

So "Lawrence" Griffith got five dollars for two days' work on a one-reel melodrama called *Rescued from the Eagle's Nest*. It showed a woodsman's baby carried off from in front of his house by a great eagle. Then the woodsman climbed a cliff to the eagle's nest, battled the bird, and rescued the child. The exteriors on the cliff were shot across the Hudson River from New York City on the cliffs of the

New Jersey Palisades. The scene outside the woodsman's cabin and the rescue of the baby from the bird's claws were shot in the Bronx studio with a painted background. The two kinds of scenes did not match up very well, and the bird looked obviously stuffed, but audiences apparently didn't notice that kind of thing.

In Porter, Griffith had met the first American cameraman-director (early on, both jobs were carried by the same man) who undertook to tell an audience stories through visual images on film. In so doing, Porter had uncovered some of the techniques through which this might be done effectively, techniques which Griffith himself has sometimes been credited with having introduced. It is perhaps hard for us to realize it today, for we are so accustomed to the techniques used to tell a story on film—both in movies and as modified in television techniques, and even in comic strips—that we barely notice those techniques. But each had to be discovered, and the discovery was sometimes hard won.

In early 1903, Edwin S. Porter had finished a film called *The Life of an American Fireman*. All newly shot footage, it was in part a kind of documentary film and in part a story film; one part made up of shots of a real fire and of real firemen at work, the other of a staged fire. Putting together all these different photographed elements, Porter hit upon some principles of film editing. The film opens with a shot of the fire chief asleep into which Porter inserted, by a photographic trick, in the upper corner of his film, a vignette of his wife and child—his dream, obviously. Then there is a close-up of a fire-alarm box as a hand opens it and pulls the alarm. Next we see, in a single long-shot, the firemen getting up, dressing hurriedly, sliding down the pole. Then we see them setting out in their horse-drawn wagons. When they pull up in front of a house, we see a mother and child at an upstairs window. The rest of the film is an account of their rescue.

Toward the end of 1903, Porter had made his famous "chase" film, *The Great Train Robbery*, the first Western, a very successful and highly influential narrative film. It starts with two desperadoes slugging a stationmaster. It ends with a chase on horseback and a gun fight between the good guys and the bad guys. The interiors are rather stagey. The actors walk or run across the screen left to right, or right to left, they move and gesture in a broad stage fashion, and of course each scene is photographed from only one point of view, with one camera position and no intercutting within a scene. Out of doors, however, the players are allowed to move toward the camera and away from it. At one point, the camera rides on top of a train to observe a fight. The camera pans, or pivots, to follow some fleeing bandits from the train into nearby woods. There is even a close-up of a bandit firing into the camera, but it is a stunt at the end of the film (or the beginning in some prints) and not a part of the action. *The Great Train Robbery* was so popular and so widely shown that it firmly established the nickelodeon as a part of big city entertainment in the United States and throughout the world. But for the next five years narrative technique in motion pictures stayed at the level of Porter's 1903 films.

One important element in Porter's early films not found in either *The Life of an American Fireman* or *The Great Train Robbery* is the trick shot or special-effect. For instance, his first comedies at the turn of the century employed stop-motion and similar stunts, whereby in *The Clown and the Alchemist,* for example, people and objects are made to seem to disappear. Porter, of course, stopped the camera, had everyone and everything stay put, removed an object or a performer, and resumed filming. Similarly, an object or an actor could be moved either a little or a lot while the camera was momentarily at rest. In such films, Porter was unquestionably inspired by the French magician-filmmaker Georges Meliès, who had staged and photographed his *The Mysterious Box* and *Voyage to the Moon* by 1898 and 1902, respectively.

When Griffith finished *Rescued from the Eagle's Nest,* his main ambition remained that of a writer, and his main condescension to the movies was an intention to write plots for them. It was evident that Edison didn't need any plots, and Griffith remembered Biograph and Mr. McCutcheon. The American Biograph Studios were in an old brownstone at 11 East 14th Street that had once been a millionaire's town house, the Cunard mansion. That meant Biograph was one of the few companies then using controlled, artificial light to photograph its interiors. Biograph had started with the "Muto-scope" machine, its own variant of the Edison Kinetoscope viewer, and when the demand for projected narrative films had risen, Biograph films met it.

Competition was high among film companies, and so was dishonesty. Patents were violated. Films were pirated. A borderline operator would steal a print of a film, strike a new negative, put new titles on it, and sell it as his own. Or he might re-shoot a few scenes and insert them, in the interests of "honesty." Biograph's solution to the problem was to paint its trademark initials, a stylized AB, on the scenery—on a wall, on woodwork, on a window, wherever. Important as it was and was to become, the Biograph Studio offered a far from handsome or inviting aspect. What had been the drawing room of the mansion made a good studio, but the big circular staircase seemed a little spooky to some and the cramped dressing rooms were mouse-infested. The floor boards creaked a bit and the bedrooms that were used for dressing rooms and storage were far from pleasant.

When Griffith presented himself and his scenarios to Biograph's general manager, "Old Man" McCutcheon, he found a genial and generous man. He was introduced to his eldest son, Wallace Mc-Cutcheon, his father's right-hand man and a Broadway actor and a Biograph film director as well. Griffith found almost instant welcome—but as an actor. So did Mrs. Griffith. She presented herself separately as Linda Arvidson because the two had decided—Griffith said—to keep their marriage a secret in case any other actors should resent two Griffiths on the same payroll.

Movie acting wasn't too difficult. The make-up was fairly simple ("remember, red photographs black," they were told). There was a brief rehearsal before each scene. There were no speeches to remember. One had to stay inside the lines on the floor that marked off the area the camera was taking in. And some days there were outdoor trips—usually over to Fort Lee, New Jersey—for exteriors. The two new performers listened and learned about the movies. And from the beginning Griffith listened hard and with obviously deep interest. Soon, his plots and scripts were also being used to produce films with titles like *The Music Master, The Stage Rustler, Ostler Joe,* and *At the Crossroads of Life.* They were good scripts, Griffith whimsically protested in later life, because "most of them were borrowed from the very best authors." But the Biograph Company was not doing well and good stories alone wouldn't help it. One problem was that it had few directors and no really good ones. It had two outstanding cameramen in Arthur Marvin (brother of Biograph's vice-president, Henry Marvin) and G. W. "Billy" Bitzer. Neither of them, however, showed any inclination to move on to direction. On a day when one of the directors fell ill, Bitzer suggested giving Griffith a try. Marvin called him to the office and asked him to take a seat.

"My brother tells me you appear to be rather interested in pictures, Mr. Griffith. How would you like to direct one?"

The actor-writer got out of his chair, crossed the room, and gazed out of a window. He did not reply. "We'll make it as easy as we can for you, Mr. Griffith, if you decide you'd like to try."

Griffith was thinking. He appreciated the confidence expressed in him, but he had had many rough years behind him and was simply in no position to jeopardize his future. If he tried directing and failed, would he be through as an actor and writer for Biograph? He expressed his reservations to Marvin.

"If I promise you," said the latter, "that if you fall down as a director, you can have your acting job back, will you put on a moving picture for us?"

"Yes, then I'd be willing."

And so in June of 1908, D. W. Griffith undertook *The Adventures of Dollie.* Rumor had it that the story was a lemon the other directors had avoided. It had to do with the kidnapping of an infant girl by a band of Gypsies. The child is hidden in a barrel which falls off the back of a wagon into a stream and drifts over some rapids before Dollie is finally rescued and restored to her parents.

Griffith cast his little film carefully. He used his wife. He persuaded the well-known stage actor Arthur Johnson to enter films to play Dollie's father; he had run into him on the street and thought he looked the part. (Johnson stayed in films and became one of the first movie "matinee idols.") He picked a location at Sound Beach, Old Greenwich, Connecticut (all of *Dollie* was to be exteriors). He motivated the kidnapping by having the father give a rebuff to the Gypsies. He told his story entirely in visuals, with no explanatory or dialogue titles. He told it in straightforward narrative style, moving from one camera set-up to the next—but at one point he cut back again to a locale we had seen earlier in the film, a most uncommon practice. And the progress of the barrel down the stream and through the rapids is shown in a succession of relatively brief shots, assembled in sequence.

Before Griffith undertook this film, he told himself that, in the last analysis, he could depend on good, clear photography to get him by. The cameraman was to be Arthur Marvin, but help was volunteered by Billy Bitzer. In later years, Bitzer remembered that:

> The cameraman was the whole works at that time, responsible for about everything except the immediate handling of the actors. It was his say not only as to whether the light was bright enough, but make-up, angles, rapidity of gestures, etc., besides having enough camera troubles of his own. . . . I agreed to help (Mr. Griffith) in every way. He needed a canvas covering for a gypsy wagon. I would get that, in fact all the props. Also I offered to condense the script for him and lay out the opportunities it had. . . . He came to my house. . . . I divided off half a dozen columns with titles—Drama, Comedy, Pathos, Pretty scenes . . . Judging the little I had caught from seeing his acting I didn't think he was going to be so hot. He

was very grateful for this and some other tips I gave him. All through the following sixteen years that I was at his side he always was not above taking advice, yes, even asking for suggestions or ideas. He always said to me, "Four eyes are better than two."

When *The Adventures of Dollie* was finished, it was assembled and shown to Mr. Marvin. At the end he said, "That's it—that's something like it, at least!" That evening Griffith went up to the roof of his building to search the sky. The predicted reappearance two years hence of Halley's Comet had been announced. All over the world, people were discussing the phenomenon, and clairvoyants everywhere were already predicting the beginning of a new era.

Four

Birth of an Artist

Film historian Richard Griffith has said that "the origins of older arts are lost in prehistory, their creators unknown or barely guessed at." But for the movies, "we have an almost complete record of the birth of an art." The creator of film art was David Wark Griffith. One commentator, Lloyd Morris, has said that Griffith "had no respect for the medium in which he was working, but his temperament compelled him to treat it as if it were an art. The result was that he made it one."

As we have seen, D. W. Griffith went into films as a last resort. And during his first few years in film, he spoke of what he was doing as a kind of game, a lark, a deception, and a temporary assignment. Yet the job possessed him. He worked twelve or sixteen hours a day, and others worked along with him willingly. Billy Bitzer, who soon became Griffith's regular photographer, told Seymour Stern, "we worked Sundays and Holidays. . . . Sixteen-hour days became a sort of schedule that there was no getting away from. . . . We got to making almost one complete 1000-ft. picture a day. . . . After the shooting was done, there was the regular stint of looking at film in the projection room. . . . D. W. Griffith was a tireless worker, but he had a way of making it interesting . . .

so that it did not seem like work." He would ask the impossible
of Bitzer, only to have Bitzer explain that the impossible was what
couldn't be done. "That's why you have to do it," Griffith would
say. And Bitzer would find a way. Then, the enthusiasm of both
men would lead them farther. "Well, come on, let's do it anyway.
I don't give a damn what anybody thinks about it," Griffith would
protest. That was the attitude through which the director discovered
his destiny and his stature.

Between 1908 and 1913 Griffith made more than four hundred
brief films, none of them over two reels in length. Some are trivial, some are pedantic, and some are little gems. There was, it
seems, at least a small discovery in technique or resource or attitude in nearly every one of them. Perhaps it was a more natural
bit of acting from one of the players or a bit of realism or a bit of
character-revealing "business." More often it was a matter of the
composition of an individual shot or the discovery of an innovative
film technique. But we should keep in mind that Griffith's innovations were never a matter of mere experimentation. They had to
work. And they did work because they conveyed character, situation, conflict, and emotion to audiences and they helped tell a story
about people.

In August of 1908, shooting *For the Love of Gold,* Griffith
asked for a change of his camera set-up in the middle of a scene.
He wanted to see things from another angle, closer to the actors.
The practice was virtually unheard of then and Griffith got what
he wanted only by demanding it.

By late October of 1908, Griffith was at work on a little version
of the Enoch Arden story called *After Many Years,* the tale of a
wife who loses her sea-faring husband in a shipwreck. She mourns
him long but eventually assumes him dead and remarries. He returns, however, and, when he observes the happy life she has
made for herself, decides not to reveal himself to her. In one scene,
the director wanted to be sure the audience saw the grief on the
wife's face and asked Bitzer to move his camera in close and show

that face. Bitzer was reluctant, not so much because there had never before been close-ups (he had even photographed some himself), but because they were virtually unheard of as a dramatic device in a narrative film. Then, when he assembled his film, Griffith, defying space, cut from the wife's distraught face to a shot of the shipwrecked husband (the object of her grief, alive!), then back to the wife. Mr. Marvin was appalled at such things. He wanted to see in full the actors he was paying for. And the audience, he said, would never be able to follow this jumping around. Griffith's response was significant. "Well," he said, "doesn't Dickens write that way?"

The very earliest moving pictures, the Edison Kinetoscopes let us say, were just that—photographed pictures that moved. Film historians and theorists do not seem to have made the point, but, consciously or not, early cinematographers were by and large working within the then-established traditions of still photography. And still photography, relatively young as it then was, had in turn borrowed its traditions—again, consciously or not—from painting.

Types of painting according to subject matter and point of view have probably existed since the beginning of the art. But in the 17th century, the French Royal Academy classified paintings into a hierarchy that included individual portraits; group portraits and "conversation pieces"—the latter a version of the group portrait in which the subjects were shown not merely posing for the painter but engaged in some activity, not necessarily conversation; "genre paintings" (scenes from daily life); and landscapes and vistas. Still photographers simply adopted those traditions, those points of view, those kinds of pictures. And so, in turn, did the early cinematographers, probably without giving the matter much thought. In the narrative movie, the cinematic equivalent of the portrait was the close-up; group portraits and conversation pieces became, in cinematic parlance, "two-shots," "group-shots," etc.; genre paintings and landscapes became various kinds of "long-shots." But in films, of course, the people or animals or vehicles or natural forces within

an individual shot could be shown in motion. And in Griffith's narrative films, the individual shot became a part of a continuous
cinematic flow, each shot with its own effect, but each also contributing cumulatively to drama.

All of which gets us a bit ahead of the story. There were two
other major traditions which informed the early narrative movie,
one theatrical, the other literary. When films began to offer vignettes
of character and then gradually began to tell stories, they were at
first directly influenced by the traditions and conventions of the
stage. But as we have seen, Edwin S. Porter himself soon discovered
that films could show many more scenes per drama than the stage,
and could use real settings not available to the stage.

It is perhaps not so surprising that Griffith, who was familiar
with both the theater and literature, should try to combine the resources of both traditions. It is surprising that his genius would
show him *how* to do it, for genius is always surprising. It is also
surprising that Griffith should prove to have had such a superb eye
for composition. He quickly developed a compositional sense equal
to that of a fine painter. And it was a compositional sense also
entirely appropriate to his medium, for he composed for figures in
motion, dramatically expressive motion, with a painter's eye. Thus
Griffith's films reintroduced elements and traditions of painting and
still photography as expressive parts of the dramatic film that was
based also on the stage and prose narrative.

At the same time, Griffith's true genius, as actress Lillian Gish
has put it, lay in his perceptions about film editing, "in his understanding of the interrelationships of separate shots, each contributing
to clarity and pace, adding substance, mood, and emotion to the bare
story outline." Jean Debrix has said that "Griffith discovered that
the *structure* of time in the cinema is not the same as the time we
are accustomed to in life, and that there exists a cinematographic
time *interval,* similar to the intervals in music and poetry. All of
which means that Griffith discovered the essence of cinematic
rhythm."

There was another discovery involved, however, one that is perhaps even more basic. Griffith had perceived that in film drama something intervenes between the actors and the audience. That something is the camera. The camera is the storyteller. But that apparent disadvantage or limitation can be made a thing of infinite advantage and resource. And the man who controls the camera, and the film images it gives him, is, or should be, the director. Look at me, Griffith said to Bitzer and Marvin in defending his first close-up. You see my face. Do you see the rest of me? You focus on my face. Isn't the background of the room out of focus for you? You do it every day. Let us let the camera do that. The audience will understand. Wait and see.

Griffith once mused, half jokingly, that he should have patented the "fade-out" that ends scenes, an invaluable device and the most fundamental terminal punctuation in screen drama. If he had tried to, he might have had a court contest of sorts on his hands, for there are precedents for the fade-out before his use of it. But as with so many of his devices, he and Billy Bitzer rediscovered it for themselves, and Griffith knew how to use it, even how to pace and to time it for best effect to close any given scene. Many of Griffith's early ideas were arrived at or worked out in conversation with his actors or other co-workers during their lunch breaks in the dingy basement at 11 East 14th Street. There, likely as not, they all sat on crates or packing cases and ate sandwiches that had been fetched by Bobby Harron, then the Biograph office-boy-of-all-help. Griffith had a wonderful capacity for soliciting help and advice with his problems and gaining the confidence and faith of those who helped him.

In a film about Edgar Allan Poe, Griffith achieved a high degree of contrast and shadow by using a window on one side of his set as his main source for light—and of course for shadows too. In February of 1909, Griffith and his players rushed into Central Park in the morning light to take advantage of a snowfall and film *A Politician's Love Story*. The early sun was still low in the sky, somewhat

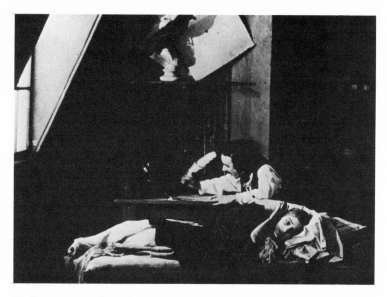

Lighting innovations in Edgar Allan Poe *(1909). Herbert Yost and Linda Arvidson.*

behind his actors, and Griffith became fascinated with the effects of this source of "back lighting" and with the long dramatic shadows cast by their bodies.* Bitzer made a further discovery about the use of such lighting. One afternoon on location in Fort Lee, New Jersey, he shot a few feet of film of a couple of the actors at lunch, with the sun directly behind them. When the film was developed and projected, he and Griffith discovered that the sun produced an intriguing halo effect around the actors' faces, but the soft reflection of the light off the white tablecloth made their features clearly visible at

---

* According to Jack Spears, Edwin S. Porter had earlier hit on that possibility, too. In his 1899 documentary on the America's Cup Race, Porter had followed the sailing yachts from the referee's boat, and at one point discovered that his camera was directly pointed toward the sun. He was later astonished at the beauty of the footage which resulted.

the same time. The two men immediately tried back lights and soft front reflectors where appropriate in their films. Other experiments with lighting effects and camera positions continued. In *A Drunkard's Reformation* and in a version of Dickens's *The Cricket on the Hearth,* for example, Griffith lit his scenes from a fireplace.

Those of us who have seen only a few early films, and seen them casually, are apt to have wrong ideas about their quality. Although the actor's art was the art of pantomime, there was always sound. The first film showings in vaudeville houses were accompanied by the theater's pit orchestra, just like the rest of the show. The humblest nickel theaters, when films found their own houses, had pianos and pianists. The larger houses, as they began to appear, had organs or even larger instrumental ensembles, sometimes up to full orchestras. And for some films in the largest theaters, sound-effects men were stationed behind the screen.

A second misconception has to do with acting. Acting styles change over the years, of course, and it is often difficult with earlier styles (as with much art from the past) to get past the surface or the conventions of the time and find the art that may be there. Griffith saw from the beginning that the broad, stylized, nineteenth-century stage style would not work on film. After all, there was no problem of "projecting" to a distant back row of the gallery. The camera was the thing to be projected to. A more subdued, intimate, and natural acting style was called for. The result of this approach was that film acting influenced all acting, that what was discovered about silent film acting affected acting on stage and later in sound films, neither of which depend on the firmness, precision, and strength of facial and bodily pantomime needed by the silent film. Griffith insisted throughout his career on a full rehearsal and complete run-through of his movies before he shot a single foot of film. Many film directors, past and present, rehearse and photograph a movie scene by scene, and often with the scenes out of order and context.

There was no "star system" in films in the beginning, incidentally.* Audiences did not know the names of the players, but they had begun to recognize their faces. When Griffith worked with Florence Lawrence and Arthur Johnson on a version of Tolstoy's *Resurrection,* Lawrence was known only as "The Biograph Girl." In *The Violin Maker of Cremona* he introduced a young actress, and audiences took to her immediately. In subsequent pictures Griffith was careful to refer to her as "Little Mary" in subtitles. The studio was flooded with mail demanding to know who she was. By the time Griffith worked with "Little Mary" (supported by an actor named Lionel Barrymore) in *The New York Hat* in 1912, Mary Pickford was ready for a lasting world fame as a movie star. By the way, the plot for that film was submitted through the mail by a young California teen-aged girl named Anita Loos. She will figure again in Griffith's story.

Griffith made in *The Curtain Pole* the first sustained American farce comedy. He was probably inspired by the film farces then being imported from France. He used the talents of Mack Sennett, a Biograph bit player who was an irrepressible cut-up off camera, but who, at the same time, observed closely directors' methods, and the business methods of the Biograph office as well. Sennett went on to become, as a director and producer, the first master of screen comedy.

In *A Convict's Sacrifice,* Griffith introduced Henry B. Walthall. But he and the other members of Griffith's growing "stock company" of players, who became so important to him and to films in general, remained anonymous. Indeed, long after "star billing" was common in promoting films, Griffiths was still reluctant to use it.

There was always color of a kind in silent films, color with special atmospheric and dramatic values. The film stock on which movies were printed for projection was not a plain, transparent plastic. It was carefully dyed in shades of blue, amber, and yellow, and red for night scenes, for indoor scenes, for bright sunlight, for

---

* For some reason, we usually speak of the "star system" as growing up with the movies. But its equivalent was well established on the stage.

"Little Mary" (*not yet Mary Pickford*) *in* The New York Hat. *From a story submitted by mail by 16-year-old Anita Loos.*

firelight, etc. Modern prints of these tinted films do not duplicate their colors, for we do not have tinted film stock any longer. Many of Griffith's masterpieces, early and late, therefore cannot be seen in their true original form. Also, there is the matter of what the photography in early films looked like. It was usually miraculously clear, crisp, and bright. But often the negative of an old film does not survive, or good prints are not found, so we are apt to know it only through foggy scratched "dupe" prints made from a substitute negative which was in turn struck second- or third-hand from a surviving print which may itself have been worn.

Finally, there is the matter of the quick, jerky movement which some people believe was prevalent in silent films. It is a purely mechanical matter. Movement in dramatic silent films was not fast and jerky. If it now seems so, the film is being projected at the wrong speed. Each film needs to be shown at the speed at which it was originally shot, and unfortunately there was no "standard" speed adhered to by companies at all periods. Indeed, the early cameras were cranked by hand, as steadily as the cameraman could do it. With sound films came the introduction of a universal, standard speed. (It was set rather arbitrarily by the Western Electric Company by the way.) The speed setting found on most modern 16 mm projectors, "silent," however, is clearly arbitrary, since there was no standard. However, deliberately fast and slow movements were sometimes mechanically created for effect in early films, particularly in comedies.

In late 1909, Biograph released a Griffith picture based on Robert Browning's poem "Pippa Passes." The film opens at dawn. For this scene, Griffith had a sliding panel built in one wall of the set and put a strong light behind it. As the camera watched Pippa sleeping, the panel was lowered and the "morning light" fell across her face. She opened her eyes and awoke as the light continued to spread and fill the room. Incidentally, *Pippa Passes* attracted a great deal of attention in the press, including the *New York Times*. It probably is safe to say that, if Griffith had made an equally good or better film on a story of his own invention, and not picked one with the built-in prestige of a Browning "classic," it would have received less attention. Indeed, it might have gone unmentioned. That is what happened with *The Lonely Villa,* released earlier in 1909. As far as we know, it appealed only to that part of its audience which was moved by it and the other filmmakers who learned much from it. In it, Griffith made some important discoveries about the resources of film and what film could do.

A woman and her two children (one of them "Little Mary") are trapped in their home by a pair of robbers who awaited the husband's departure. She manages to get a phone call to her husband partially completed before the crooks cut the wires. The husband rushes to the rescue. Griffith intercut shots of the robbers approaching the house, the terror of the wife and children, of the husband

Frames from The Lonely Villa (*1909*).

departing, then of the two ends of the phone conversation, the husband's rush back to the house and the terror inside. Griffith had defied time and space with dramatic effect. Further, with a fine sense of pace and tension, Griffith, as the action quickens, made each return to each scene increasingly shorter, until his climax.

A Corner in Wheat is a brief and, in some respects, crude depiction of a Frank Norris tale of a business tycoon who cornered the wheat market, drove up the price of bread, and caused great hardship among the poor—a film of social conscience and social problems, and one of the earliest. In one sequence, the poor are seen lined up at a baker's counter buying bread. Intercut are scenes of stock profiteers in the grain markets. Back to the baker, who hangs out a sign which announces a price increase. Some customers dejectedly drop out of the line. Subsequently, the successful tycoon celebrates his stock market victory in a lavish and somewhat wild party, and Griffith intercuts shots of the revels with a shot of the bread line in which his actors are standing still, frozen, frustrated, like dead men, their lives cut off. Many years later, well into the 1950s, the "freeze frame" commonly reappeared with similar dramatic effect.

By early 1910, Griffith had explored locations in New Jersey, Connecticut, and New York State (some of the last in a town with the marvelous name of Cuddiebackville). He would seek them out perhaps because of stories he had in mind, and they, in turn, might suggest other stories to him. An old house might inspire a Revolutionary War tale. A terrain might suggest a rural tale. But winter in the Northeast was often prohibitive for outdoor filming, and Griffith wanted new locales.

The Biograph company had become a leader—because of Griffith's work, of course. But southern California was becoming increasingly attractive to filmmakers because of the warm weather, the sunshine, and the variety of natural settings (mountains, plains, valleys, shoreline). One could shoot without artificial light, with only a sheet of muslin over the open-to-the-sky top of the set to diffuse the sunlight. Some companies even wandered out to a barely settled Los Angeles suburb called Hollywood. So, beginning in early 1910, Griffith and his actors and crew made the first of several winter trips to the West Coast, a rather long and not exactly comfortable train trip in those days.

A film called *The Lonedale Operator* from March of 1911 is, in one sense, a return to the principles Griffith discovered in *The Lonely Villa*. In another sense, it is a synthesis of all that Griffith had discovered about narrative movies involving melodramatic suspense. Blanche Sweet, telegraph operator in the Lonedale station, is held captive by a pair of crooks. She manages to tap out a message to the next station for her father and sweetheart, both of whom are railroad men. They commandeer a train and rush to her rescue. One immediately noticeable thing about *The Lonedale Operator* is that the actors do not begin their action after they enter the frame. They are in meaningful action when we first encounter them. Again, Griffith employed exceptionally effective cross-cutting, switching from the girl to her rescuers in progressively shorter lengths of film. But he also moved in closer to the train, to its smokestack, to its screaming whistle (well, one can *almost* hear it scream), and to its churning wheels each time. Film historian Lewis Jacobs has commented, "Griffith uses every opportunity for emphasizing movement. Not only was there action within the shot, but the camera itself moved. . . . The cutting back and forth from the speeding train to the captive gave momentum to the whole. The fluency of action which Griffith achieved by these devices brought a new kinetic quality to the screen."

Griffith had clearly developed another characteristic by the time this film was made: even in the most complex balanced composition, perhaps involving several actors, he could draw our attention to the smallest detail—a face, a stance, an object—while still letting us take in the whole.

The quality of the California coastline again suggested the Enoch Arden story to Griffith. But in returning to it, he had more

The homecoming, Enoch Arden *(1911), in two reels.*

in mind than reusing a plot that had interested him earlier. He wanted to make a two-reel film, a movie that would have to be distributed in two cans. The Biograph front office screamed hysterically at that one. Each refinement in technique was already costing them more and more money per film. Griffith was using up film stock at a pretty high rate in order to photograph all those angles and do all that cutting, and he was filling up every inch of their 1000-foot reels. Yes, he brought them in money and prestige. But he was also a fanciful spendthrift. And, anyway, audiences wouldn't sit still that long, for two whole reels, to see just one story. They struck a compromise. Griffith could make his two-reel picture. But Biograph would release it and rent it in two parts. The patrons gave Biograph their answer and justified Griffith: they clamored to see *Enoch Arden* whole at one showing. The two-reel film became established fare.

Five

From Biograph
to Majestic

Among his associates, and behind his back, Griffith was "the Chief" or "D.W." But to his face, he was always "Mr. Griffith." It did not occur to anyone to call him anything else. To some his voice had an almost hypnotic quality. He never seemed to raise it on the set, and his manner seemed easy and unobtrusive, yet with an undercurrent of high enthusiasm that inspired everyone. This quality had a special meaning for his actors, for it was possible for him to coach and encourage them continuously during the filming. He remained, most of the time and with most of his actresses, the courtly Southern gentleman. With most, but not with all. For as no man's character is without its shadow side, no man's manners are without their imperfections. He once became exasperated with Blanche Sweet after hours of fruitless encouragement, and gave her a bent knee as though he were kicking her off the set. Then, as he usually did when he was under tension, Griffith burst into song, apparently oblivious of a difficult situation.

When Mary Pickford (born Gladys Smith) had first presented herself at Biograph on a bright May morning in 1909, she announced that she was an accomplished actress and an artist, had worked for the great theatrical producer David Belasco in fact, and might be

interested in working in pictures for a while if the salary were satisfactory. Well, the answer came back, we do need a type like you in
a picture we have planned. We pay $5 a day when you work. Be-
neath Miss Pickford's attractive curls, there was the mind of both
an actress and a shrewd businesswoman. That mind immediately
went into operation. "What!," she countered, "I must have at least
ten!"

Miss Pickford later felt that Griffith had been boorish and hate-
ful to her on their first meeting. He did not seem impressed with
her. In her screen test and her early film work, he said her acting
was wooden and that she was overweight. Then he invited her to
dinner, which shocked her. However, he sensed the unique screen
personality, the quality of innocence plus strength, which Mary
Pickford projected, for he persuaded the Biograph office to meet her
terms and to keep her on when they had found her first films un-
impressive.

Still, the two squabbled; Griffith squabbled with Pickford as
with no one else. He once lost his temper with her during the filming of a scene, whereupon she bit him while her sister, Lottie Pickford, pulled his ears from behind. At other times Griffith openly
compared her work unfavorably with that of some of his other
actresses. Once he gave a role to young Mae Marsh for which Miss
Pickford thought she had been picked. On another occasion, he even
shoved her in anger and she fell to the floor, and Bobby Harron,
now promoted from office boy to actor, threatened to quit. After
such quarrels, Miss Pickford herself would usually quit. Griffith
would apologize abjectly. And she would return.

Sometimes there was method in the director's actions. Once,
when he felt that Little Mary was not registering enough anger, he
insulted her leading man, Owen Moore, as both an actor and a man.
Miss Pickford became furious. "Shoot it, Billy! Shoot it!," Griffith
ordered Bitzer, and he got his footage of Little Mary in a rage.
Griffith had known that she was secretly married to Owen Moore
at the time. Still, Griffith and Mary Pickford had stimulating and

beneficial discussions about movies and movie making. She let him know she thought he let his players overact. And she was interested in all aspects of making films. "I used to watch him at work for hours. It was fascinating, especially when he'd come up with some exciting innovation. Whenever he would say, 'What do you think, Pickford?,' I felt complimented, yet I believe he didn't really care what others thought."

One actress whose name Griffith had invoked to taunt Miss Pickford was Blanche Sweet. He gave her the lead in *The Battle*, another important early film. For it, Griffith reverted to a one-reel story, but he told a Civil War tale with The Boy and The Girl, and some realistic battle scenes and vivid use of crowds. Another actress whose name Griffith used against Miss Pickford was Lillian Gish. Of all Griffith's early discoveries, she was the one with whom he had the most important and lasting relationship. She and her sister Dorothy came to Griffith one day in the early summer of 1912. Each was still in her teens. They had, in their mother's care, several years of treading the boards of American theaters behind them. The Gish sisters were friends of Mary Pickford and her mother, and she had suggested Biograph to them. Movies needed very young girls, even for leading ladies then, to insure that they did not photograph like dowagers. Griffith came upon the Gish sisters seated affectionately side by side on a bench in the hall of the Biograph building. Lillian seemed etherially pretty, and Dorothy pert, saucy, and full of mischief. But nevertheless he decided he could not tell them apart by name, so he put a pink ribbon on Dorothy and a blue one on Lillian.

To Lillian, Griffith was tall, imposing, vigorous, with a penetrating eye and a nose that was much too large. She spoke up and told him she and her sister were "of the theater" and friends of Miss Pickford. Griffith turned to Mary Pickford. "You have courage to introduce me to two such pretty girls. Aren't you afraid of losing your job? You'll be sorry." The director then called in Henry B. Walthall, Lionel Barrymore, Harry Carey, Elmer Booth, and Bobby

THE BATTLE

An Influence that Makes the Hero

IN THE DAYS OF '61 how many of the brave soldiers were urged to deeds of valor and heroism by thoughts of "the girl he left behind". This story tells of the transforming of a pusillanimous coward into a lion-hearted hero by the derision of the girl he loved. The battle takes place outside her home, and he, panic-stricken, rushes in, trembling with fear, to hide. She laughs in scorn at his cowardice and commands him to go back and fight. Her fortitude inspires him and he manages to rejoin his company before his absence is noticed. Ammunition is low and somebody must take the hazardous journey to procure more from another regiment, which he volunteers to do. This undertaking cannot be adequately described, for the young man faces death at every turn. The most thrilling part of his experience is where the opposing forces build bonfires along the road to menace the powder-wagon. This, without question, is the most stirring war picture ever produced.

Released Nov. 6, 1911

The Biograph Bulletin for The Battle, *dated Nov. 6, 1911.*

Harron to observe, and immediately gave the Gishes the situation of a film he was planning called *The Unseen Enemy.* "Tell the camera what you feel, Miss Blue. Fear—*more fear.* Look into the lens!" Before he was through, the director was firing a gun at the ceiling. Lillian was sure he had gone mad. And then he stopped. He was completely calm. He told them it would make a wonderful scene. They had expressive faces and bodies. Would they like to be in the picture? They would.

In late October of 1913, Biograph released a realistic, extraordinarily photographed, vividly acted (down to the smallest extra and background part), and charming film called *The Musketeers of Pig Alley,* with Lillian Gish and Elmer Booth. "Charming" may seem an odd word to apply to it when one learns that it had to do with small-time gangsters in the big city (it has been called the first "gangster film"), but the film does have charm, too, and pointing that out indicates the complexity of effect Griffith was able to achieve in it. There is even a redemption, in the end, of one of the crooks, a part played with verve by Booth. *The Musketeers of Pig Alley* remains one of the most intrinsically and lastingly artistic of all the Biographs.

The fact that Bitzer achieved such stunning images as can be seen in this film is something of a miracle in itself. The Mutoscope, the camera used by Biograph, was a far from ideal instrument. It could not rewind the film, for one thing; therefore certain double-exposure tricks which were very popular with audiences could not be done. Perhaps the Biograph bosses became reconciled with Griffith's close-ups, his framing devices, and his montage cutting because they thought of them as competing photographic novelties rather than dramatic resources. Raw film was put into the Mutoscope camera without today's sprocket holes; the camera itself punched out two holes per frame as the film stock passed through. Punched out pieces of celluloid fell to the floor. Static electricity built up in the camera and often spoiled the film with streaks of "light," particularly on location and in cold weather. An alcohol lamp, which

Lillian Gish, Elmer Booth, and Harry Carey in The Musketeers of Pig Alley.

warmed the camera, helped control the cold-weather static electricity that caused the streaks.

The film was "unbacked," that is, it had not been coated on its reverse side with a light-absorbing material, so it exaggerated highlights and spread them brightly. This effect could be used dramatically, of course, but there were many times when one might not want it. The highlights could be toned down by putting a hood over the camera lens. Once Bitzer improvised such a hood with a glue pot, but the developed film proved to have its corners rounded off darkly, framing its center in a circle. Griffith, not unexpectedly, became very excited and wanted to use the effect. The next step involved putting an iris on the hood which could be opened and closed for effect—as a substitute "fade out" at the end of a scene or as a kind of "fade in" at the beginning.

And one of the remarkable street scenes from the same film.

For *The Massacre,* released only a few days after *The Musketeers of Pig Alley,* Griffith once again angered the Biograph executives. He went far over his budget in a determination to go beyond anything he had done yet. His story had to do with General Custer's last stand, and he made of it the first important American film spectacle. He used cast, costumes, sets, and crowds on a large scale. There were mass scenes, extreme long shots of panoramic views, detailed shots of close fighting, all edited in rapid, telling continuity. And he used what came to be called the "running insert" by placing his camera in an open "touring car," as they were then called, and shooting directly at charging horsemen.

But *The Massacre* went largely unnoticed. Something singular had happened to motion pictures in the United States. Several celebrated European actresses had consented to appear in films, films of three, four, and even five reels. Chief among them was Sarah Bernhardt in a version of *Queen Elizabeth*. Bernhardt's film was imported by a young penny arcade and nickelodeon operator named Adolph Zukor and released in prestige theater locations to great acclaim. On the strength of its success, Zukor announced a new company, "Famous Players in Famous Plays," films of four reels to be produced with name performers from the theater. Whereas Griffith's *The Musketeers of Pig Alley* and *The Massacre* seem cinematic miracles today, Bernhardt's *Queen Elizabeth* seems an impossibly crude, stilted, and stagey film, important only because it is a record of sorts of an important stage actress.

Griffith, one commentator has observed, was a master of boiling the pot when pot boilers were called for. He spent a great deal of 1913 in California, meeting Biograph's schedule with short fare. But early in the year, his leadership received another blow with the release of a spectacular costume and religious film from Italy, *Quo Vadis*. It was eight reels long. When it was imported, it proved too big for the nickelodeons and was shown across the country in big "legitimate" houses at $1 admission with great success.

Griffith's ambition was now reinforced by a bitter determination to reestablish his leadership. He planned a film spectacle but kept its subject a secret. He moved his players north of Los Angeles to Chatsworth. Griffith's associates were quite intrigued. He had never before been so exacting, done so much careful rehearsing, shot so much film, used so many camera set-ups, done so much re-shooting, used such crowds, such huge sets, and such costumes. When done, Griffith had one of the first American four-reel films, an extravagant treatment of a tale from the Biblical Apocrypha and a play by Thomas Bailey Aldrich, *Judith of Bethulia*. The plot tells how Holofernes, Nebuchadnezzar's general (played by Henry B. Walthall, a small man, magically made large by Bitzer's camera), laid siege to the Israelite city of Bethulia. The inhabitants, near starvation, were ready to surrender. Judith, a young widow (played by Blanche Sweet), conceived a bold plan. She first prostrated herself and prayed for God's forgiveness. Then she dressed herself seductively, stole into Holofernes' camp, spent the night with him in feasting and revelry, and then beheaded the general. In the battle that followed, Holofernes' troops were demoralized without his leadership, and they lost. In one subplot, Bobby Harron and Mae Marsh played young Bethulian lovers; in another Lillian Gish was a young mother desperately seeking food to save her baby. Griffith told his story in four movements, so to speak, four sub-climaxes before the final resolution. It was a structure he had used before in *Pippa Passes,* and an idea he was to develop further in *Intolerance.* *Judith of Bethulia* was full of colorful mass scenes in huge sets, but it had intimate scenes as well. There were stormings of the city walls, chariot charges, and the destruction of the enemy camp by fire. Religious spectacle on film in America has its origins here.

Day by day, the Biograph office in New York had been outraged at the cost sheets sent in from California by the company accountant "Little" Epping. And when Griffith returned to New York to the fine new Biograph studios in the Bronx (studios still being used into the 1970s, by the way) to complete shooting of his interior scenes, he found depressing news awaiting him. Executives had decided that henceforth films would be more stage-oriented—that's where success lay. Anyway, Griffith was undisciplined and a spendthrift. Biograph had hired the theatrical producers Klaw and Erlanger to make films. Griffith would have the job of supervising production but would not be allowed to direct. *Judith* might be released, but in four separate parts.

Griffith was angry and bitter and, he was sure, totally misunderstood by his employers. It was time to leave. A new alliance had formed in California between the Reliance and Majestic production companies and the Mutual distributing company. Griffith would join them. He left Biograph October 1, 1913. Biograph finally released *Judith* in 1914, but by then imported spectacle films were

Mae Marsh as Naomi, the woman at the well in Judith of Bethulia
(*1913*).

fairly common, and Griffith himself had moved on to other and
more important projects that involved him even more deeply.

The question of the relationship of stage to screen had been
raised anew by recent events and Griffith was prepared to answer
it specifically at the time. He did not think that a knowledge of
stagecraft was necessary to a command of movie directing. "The
stage," he said, "is a development of centuries, based on certain
fixed conditions and within prescribed limits. It is needless to point
out what these are. The moving picture, although a growth of only
a few years, is boundless in its scope and endless in its possibilities.

. . . The conditions of the two arts being different, it follows that the requirements are equally dissimilar. . . ." And Griffith also said, most succinctly, "The task I am trying to achieve is above all to make you see."

When he left Biograph, Griffith took with him his "stock company" of players and even certain technical and business people. He had Billy Bitzer under personal contract. Bitzer, however, didn't go willingly, even with an offer from Griffith of triple his Biograph salary. He did not believe that the new company would stand for Griffith's consumption of money and raw film stock any more than Biograph had. Among the inducements Griffith made to him was, "We will bury ourselves in hard work out at the coast for five years, and make the greatest pictures ever made, make a million dollars, and retire, and then you can have all the time you want to fool around with your camera gadgets, etc., and I shall settle down to write."

"Now," thought Bitzer, "how can he be so sure of that . . . ?"

Before he set out for California, Griffith rented a loft near Union Square, put his carpenters to work on a set or two, and made a five-reel film in four days. It was frankly designed to make money for the new company, and even its title was aimed at the box office, *The Battle of the Sexes*. It had to do with a straying husband (Owen Moore), a homewrecker, and a daughter (Lillian Gish) who was driven to commit murder to relieve her mother's suffering. Also featured were Robert Harron and Donald Crisp. Griffith then shot some New York street footage to be used in a film to be called *The Escape*.

When he arrived in California with his company (Reliance-Majestic had had to pawn one of its pictures to get them there), Griffith set to work fulfilling his main function to the new company, that of keeping the assembly line rolling and training directors and actors. He was credited with supervising a series of comedies for Dorothy Gish, but he privately admitted he was little concerned with anyone's films but his own. He, or his studio, supervised or trained Chester and Sidney Franklin, Raoul Walsh, Donald Crisp, Elmer Clifton, George Siegmann, and others, in direction. He found a durable star in Wallace Reid. He finished *The Escape,* based on a sensational contemporary play by Paul Armstrong about eugenics and crime, with Blanche Sweet, Mae Marsh, and Robert Harron. The picture was not well received in its time and is now among the lost Griffith features. He put together a film in several short episodes called *Home Sweet Home,* featuring most of his players and revolving around a fictionalized version of the life of songwriter John Howard Payne and the supposed effect of his songs on the lives of others. The first of the film's sequences, "Apple Pie Mary," a light comedy with Mae Marsh and Robert Harron, is by far the best.

Griffith also made an interesting feature called *The Avenging Conscience,* based on writings of Edgar Allan Poe. In his book *The Art of the Moving Picture,* Vachel Lindsay, the American poet, called it "an example of that rare thing, a use of old material that is so inspired that it has the dignity of a new creation." In *The Films of D. W. Griffith,* Edward Wagenknecht praises the provocative effectiveness of most of *The Avenging Conscience,* but he also points out the incongruous awkwardness of some of it. An early sequence at a garden party, shot on a large estate, had no intrinsic relationship to the rest of the film, its characters, or their conflicts. Still, Griffith undertook a largely psychological pursuit in *The Avenging Conscience* and not merely an action-filled chase. Subtitles announce that the film was "Suggested by Edgar Allan Poe's story of 'The Telltale Heart' and by certain of his poems of the affections" and was "An humble effort to express, in motion picture form, the psychology of conscience, the great safeguard of human righteousness."

The core of the plot has to do with an orphaned nephew and his guardian-uncle who is ambitious for his ward, and is convinced that his budding romance with a village girl can damage a very promising future. Frustrated, the nephew apparently murders the uncle and walls him into a fireplace. As the nephew is questioned by a

Henry B. Walthall and The Avenging Conscience (*1914*).

detective investigating the uncle's disappearance, Griffith rapidly and vividly portrays his agitation at the beat of a pendulum in a wall clock and at the tapping of the detective's pencil and foot. These are likened, in a subtitle, to the beating of the dead man's heart. The scene is climaxed by the scream of an owl outside the window. All conveyed, of course, without sound effects, in visuals and pantomime. The ending, in which it is revealed that the murder had been the nephew's dream, or perhaps his moral vision inspired by a reading of Poe, is perhaps a disappointment but it is Griffith's effort to affirm a positive didactic effect for Poe's works. Lindsay calls this final scene a "conscience-climax" that is "reached by dramatization of *The Tell-tale Heart* reminiscence in the memory of a dreaming man."

Interspersed are various symbolic scenes and quotations from Poe. When the nephew is ordered to stay at home and work instead of meeting his love, a title shows us a stanza from *To One in Paradise*. Before his confession, the young man sees himself, his face frozen in horror before a door which he compulsively opens to let in the "ghouls" from Poe's *The Bells*. At "the birth of an evil thought" Griffith introduces visuals and titles which depict nature as "one long system of murder" in which a spider in her web devours a fly and ants in turn annihilate the spider. Lindsay comments on these shots that "their horror and decorative iridescence are of the Poe sort. It is the first hint of the Poe hieroglyphic we have had, except for the black patch over the eye of the uncle, along with his jaundiced, cadaverous face. The boy meditates on how all nature turns on cruelty, and on the survival of the fittest."

Thus, Griffith was involved in a complex of projects for Reliance-Majestic in 1914—directing four films in as many months, as well as executing dozens of supervisory and production projects. But it was not with any of these that his heart lay. For he was also involved in a project entirely his own, one he spoke of and worked at with more dedication, energy, and seriousness than he had given even to *Judith of Bethulia*. He was decidedly not "grinding out another sausage."

Six

The Birth of a Nation

In the early spring of 1914, Frank Woods, a scenario writer with Griffith's company, urged the director to take a look at Thomas W. Dixon's novel, *The Clansman*—or take another look, for Griffith had known of Dixon's play based on the novel. Woods was enthusiastic about the movie possibilities for the book. Indeed the company with which Woods had formerly been associated, the Kinemacolor corporation (which produced color films, as its name implies), had tried a movie version of the successful stage play based on the book, but had left it uncompleted. Griffith also looked at another of Dixon's books, a view of the Reconstruction period titled *The Leopard's Spots*.

The material began to take form in his own mind as a film. He began research. Within a relatively short time, he was ready to take aside several members of his company and say, "After the others leave today, would you please stay?" He spoke to Lillian Gish, Mae Marsh, Henry B. Walthall, Bobby Harron, Miriam Cooper, Elmer Clifton, George Siegmann, Walter Long, and others, and when they assembled, he told them that he was going to produce a film that would tell the truth about the War Between the States. "The history books did not." His story would concern two families, the Stonemans from the North and the Camerons from the South. He swore his cast to secrecy. If other companies heard about the project they would rush into production with films on the same subject before he could finish his.

When he did finish, Griffith had fairly transformed Dixon's material. He had a new title, *The Birth of a Nation.* And he had a film of imaginative power, vast scope and superb, fluid technique, and one which earned for the screen the status of an art.

Production began on a scale that was both intimate and huge. Griffith researched his project in history books, in maps, and in his own memory. He studied old photographs, particularly those by Mathew Brady. (Bitzer bribed a lady librarian with a box of chocolates to get copies of Brady's shots.) He reproduced the interior of Ford's Theater to re-stage the assassination of Abraham Lincoln, and even got a copy of the play Lincoln was attending, *Our Ameri-*

Ford's Theater. "Sic Semper Tyrannis." *And John Wilkes Booth flees the assassination of a President.*

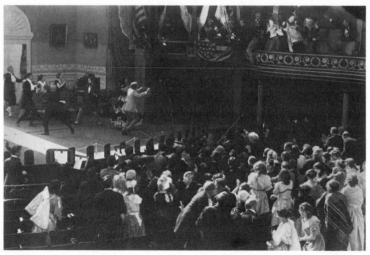

can Cousin, and had it acted out on his stage. His quest for authenticity led him to instruct his carpenters to reproduce exactly the large, paneled interior of the South Carolina legislature, and he himself searched the California countryside for a landscape that looked like the battlefields outside of Petersburg, Virginia. He built roads, even dug streams and laid out brooks.

Griffith kept the whole film in his head. He had no script, and as far as we know kept no written notes. He put his company through weeks of exacting rehearsals. But as the supreme intuitive artist, he improvised on the spur of the moment as well. Noticing a group of extras on a hillside having lunch one day, he hit upon the idea of showing us (on a partly masked screen) a family huddled on a hillside in a shot that then irised out to reveal Northern troops ransacking and burning their farmhouse below. When he noticed the way Lillian Gish's blonde hair fell when she was picked up by one of the actors during rehearsal, he recast her role in the film.

He shot for nine weeks. He rented land equal in size to an entire county. He used hundreds of extras. He shot vast panoramas and intimate close-ups. He directed marches, battles, sackings, and huge rides on horseback, calling directions through a megaphone and using a system of relayed signals across the landscape. He staged intimate love scenes. Bitzer photographed it all with one Pathé camera. And he got unheard-of effects. For one sequence involving a huge charge of horses, Griffith wanted close-ups of the flying feet of their mounts. Bitzer crouched on the ground amid the dust and sod. The side of his Pathé was kicked in, but he got the shot.

Griffith ran out of money. Financing became more than Reliance-Majestic-Mutual could carry, so he and Harry Aitken formed a separate company, the Epoch Producing Company. His cast came to work one morning to discover Griffith was missing—an unheard of thing. He appeared after lunch, looking weary, and went to work. On the next payday there were no checks for the cast. The money was gone.

Frame blow-ups from the battle footage.

Most of our knowledge of Griffith's money-raising activities for this film comes from his actors and, as Robert M. Henderson has revealed, Griffith preferred to have his actors believe he was personally raising money that was in fact chiefly the product of Harry Aitken's persuasiveness and ingenuity, first with bankers in New York and second with voluntary small investors in California. Griffith and Aitken tried theater owners, department store owners, store customers, the regular patrons of a small lunchroom near the Majestic studios—anyone. Griffith once rushed into the city room of the *Los Angeles Times,* trying to raise $250 to meet his payroll. The word was out in the film business that Griffith had become more foolish than ever, for, in spending so much, he had priced himself out of success for his film. Even if the public did like it, the gossip said the movie could not possibly earn back its cost, much less make a profit.

But Griffith remained calm and kept his problems to himself, faithful to a creative urge that simply had to be expressed. He had his film finished in February of 1915. Finished, edited, tinted, printed, and with an instrumental score by Griffith and Joseph Carl Breil compiled of familiar and traditional material as well as a few original themes, to be played by theater orchestras. He had a film in two parts that ran three hours, which he trimmed slightly to two hours and forty-five minutes during initial screenings. He opened it at Clune's Auditorium in Los Angeles for $2 a ticket. (Clune had been an investor.) The first audiences to see the film were so overcome that they sat silent, but they soon leaped to their feet and cheered.

Griffith now became his own promotion man. He played *The Birth of a Nation* at $2 in large, mostly "legitimate" houses. Audiences flocked to it and applauded. No one had known people could be so moved by a motion picture. Critics appeared to praise the film where there had been no critics before. It made a fortune. It brought new prestige and popularity to the movies, changed their whole method of presentation. Huge new movie theaters and chains of theaters were built, and huge production companies were formed, on the basis of its success. It made D. W. Griffith the foremost artist of a new art.

The Birth of a Nation opens with a scene of slave-trading, "the seeds of dis-union," a subtitle explains. The traffic in black men is being blessed by a minister in Puritan-like garb (therefore apparently Northern) as "God's will." Next we are briefly shown the Abolitionist movement, again led by Northern ministers. The film then turns to its story proper. Phil and Ted Stoneman of Pennsyl-

Henry B. Walthall leads a charge in The Birth of a Nation.

vania visit their friends from boarding school, the Camerons, in Piedmont, South Carolina. Phil Stoneman falls in love with Margaret Cameron, and Ben Cameron (Henry B. Walthall) is much taken with a daguerreotype of Phil's sister, Elsie Stoneman (Lillian Gish). The Civil War breaks out. The Stoneman sons enlist with the Union forces, the Camerons with the Confederates. Two younger Cameron sons and Ted Stoneman are killed in the fighting. Piedmont is ruined and pillaged. Ben Cameron ("the little Colonel") is wounded and becomes Phil Stoneman's prisoner. In a prison hospital, he is nursed by Elsie Stoneman. With Elsie's help, Mrs. Cameron intervenes with President Lincoln ("the great heart") for Ben's life. We learn that the Honorable Austin Stoneman, the father of Elsie and the Stoneman boys, is a power in Congress and is in favor of a program of punishment and even revenge toward the South. "Their leaders must be hanged and the states treated like conquered provinces," reads one title, and at another point Stoneman reveals his obsession to "put the white South under the heel of the black South." He intends to make a mulatto, Silas Lynch, "a leader of the people." (Griffith obviously based his Stoneman on Thaddeus Stevens—or on one view of Stevens's words and

The Little Colonel (Henry B. Walthall) and Elsie Stoneman (Lillian Gish) in The Birth of a Nation. *A romance threatened by war.*

Elsie Stoneman (Lillian Gish). From the hospital scenes in The Birth of a Nation.

actions at any rate.) Lincoln refuses to approve such a policy of revenge. The South surrenders at Appomattox, and very soon after, Lincoln is assassinated. With this catastrophe, Griffith ended the first section of his film.

The second half is concerned with Reconstruction. The South is in chaos, and Northern opportunists ("carpetbaggers") move in to exploit it, and to exploit the newly freed slaves. Stoneman quietly gains power, and, with Phil and Elsie, he moves to the South, to Piedmont, to administer his program of "equality" for Negroes. He rents a house next to the Stonemans. Elsie and Ben become engaged. The state is looted. Lawlessness runs riot. Ben Cameron organizes an "invisible empire" of vigilantes, the Clansmen (admittedly the historical Ku Klux Klan), who play upon superstition to enforce law and order. Gus, a mulatto renegade (Walter Long in black-face), becomes a hanger-on with the black "militia" of Silas Lynch, who has been made Lieutenant Governor in a rigged election. Gus makes advances to the youngest Cameron daughter, Flora. She flees through the woods to escape him and, in despair, hurls herself off a cliff. Ben discovers her, dying. The Cameron father is arrested for harboring a Clansman. Phil Stoneman, shocked at the evident corruption and chaos produced by his father's policies, helps rescue him, and he, with the other Camerons and their few faithful servants, takes refuge in a cabin. There they are attacked by the militia. Elsie Stoneman hurries to Silas Lynch to intervene for them. Lynch locks her in a room and says he will help them if she will marry him. Faced with this harrowing dilemma, Elsie collapses. Austin Stoneman, now confronted with the consequence of his policies, turns against Lynch. The climax (based in part on Griffith's Biograph *The Battle at Elderbush Gulch*) is a massive gathering and ride of the Clansmen, headed by Ben. They mow down the militia, take Lynch, free both Elsie and Stoneman, and finally ride to save the Camerons in their cabin. Out of this resolution, a title announces, a new nation is born.

The critic and poet James Agee has said that Griffith's genius was that he was "a great primitive poet, a man capable, as only great primitive artists can be, of intuitively perceiving and perfecting the tremendous magical images that underlie the memory and imagination of entire peoples." He also said that all through the work "there are images which are as impossible to forget, once you have seen them, as some of the grandest and simplest passages in music or poetry." This might be said to apply to every shot in the battle scenes in *The Birth of a Nation*. First, they are beautiful, and, second, they seem real. Yet there is no hypocrisy in them, for Griffith is one of the few filmmakers who have been able to make war seem exactly what it is—at once huge, heroic, pathetic, wasteful,

The Little Colonel in the trenches.

harrowing, cruel, degrading, and horrifying. Griffith's battle scenes have been imitated in films ever since, but they have probably never been equalled in their complexity.

The images of fighting are only a few of the scenes in this film that one does not forget. There is the "iris out" from a huddled group of a mother and her two daughters hiding on a hillside in the upper left of the screen; the frame opens up and the camera pans to reveal Sherman's army burning this family's farm on its scorched-earth march to the sea. The effect could never have been achieved had Griffith cut from a shot of the mother and daughters to a shot of the troops, or had he shown us all of the scene without the opening iris. Then, there is the famous homecoming of Ben Cameron after the war to Piedmont. First we see the empty and ravaged street. Then his figure, slightly bent, moves slowly to the steps of his scarred home. He is greeted eagerly, pathetically, by his little sister (Mae Marsh) who had been a child when he departed and is now virtually a young woman. Then, as he enters the house, comes an encircling arm about his shoulders—his mother, we know, although we never see her.

Henry B. Walthall's and Mae Marsh's are but two of the several superb performances in this film. When Ben Cameron decides to form the Clan, Walthall lets us know that he feels their activities are both necessary and, at the same time, a torment to him. The part of Flora is at first taken by a child actress but, when Miss Marsh

Frame blow-ups of battle charge.

An "iris-out" on Sherman's march to the sea from The Birth of a Nation.

takes over, it remains all of a piece. And her girlish combination of fear, excitement, and even delight, as black troops headed by a scalawag captain raid Piedmont, is remarkable. Even the historical re-creations, like Lincoln's assassination, are apt to affect us, not as if we are seeing a vivid film on the event, but as if we are actually there.

Above all there is the flow of this film's major sequences. "From the very beginning," Lewis Jacobs has commented, "shots are merged into a flux. Either the actions within shots have some kind of movement or the duration of shots is so timed that the effect is one of continuous motion. The motion creates a 'beat' which accents the relationships of the separate elements of the film and produces a single, powerful effect." Indeed, one of the movie's earliest critics, Henry MacMahon, writing in the *New York Times* in 1915, remarkably perceived the achievement of Griffith's editing. He wrote, "Every little series of pictures, continuing from four to fifteen seconds, symbolizes a sentiment, a passion, or an emotion. Each successive series, similar yet different, carries the emotion to the next higher power, til at last, when both of the parallel emotions have attained the nth power, so to speak, they meet in the final swift shock of victory and defeat."

It is surely significant that *The Birth of a Nation,* the first generally accepted work of art in the American film, should be so deeply connected with the most painful episode in American history and with our most terrible and unresolved problems. Liberals denounced it. The National Association for the Advancement of Colored People decried it. It was picketed and attacked. There were

The Little Colonel's homecoming from The Birth of a Nation.

fights and riots. Griffith protested that it was all true, that neither
it nor he was anti-Negro. And he ended by declaring himself for
an absolutely free screen, denouncing all efforts at movie censorship.
But the film did stir up deep trouble, terrible misunderstanding,
and it gave impetus to a revived Ku Klux Klan, whose stated purposes and intentions were somewhat different from, and more
overtly white supremacist than, those of the original.

Woodrow Wilson said that *The Birth of a Nation* was like history written by lightning, and Woodrow Wilson was an outstanding
American historian before he was a President. But it may be relevant
that Woodrow Wilson was also a white Southerner. *The Birth of
a Nation* is, however, not primarily history; it is drama, it is art,
and, like all art, its purpose is to give life meaning. Much art gives
meaning to man's inner, emotional life—even some art which *seems*
to deal with the outer world and man's position in that world.
There can be no question that *The Birth of a Nation* puts experience into order. Indeed, its very theme is the restoration of personal
and social order on both an intimate and a grand scale. Perhaps we
should see it as just such a drama and, as with Shakespeare's
Richard III, not worry over whether or not it is good history. But
The Birth of a Nation repeatedly insists that it *is* history. Griffith
inserts title after title to tell us in effect that "it's all true." Is it, as
Woodrow Wilson implied, good history? Or even valid interpretation of history? Is it perhaps a valid interpretation if one grants that
it has its scapegoats? And clearly its scapegoats are blacks: American Negroes and American mulattoes.

James Agee has said that Griffith was making a penetrating and
sincere effort to understand, much more so that the liberals who
have condemned his film. Agee said that there are in the film
"degrees of understanding, honesty, and compassion far beyond the
capacity of his accusers." But the historical facts of the so-called
Reconstruction years were beyond Griffith as much as they were
beyond his detractors.

There can be no question that Griffith's effort was more temperate than Dixon's. Dixon's *The Clansman* is full of the vilest racism. One frequently quoted passage reviles Negroes as "thick lipped, spindle-shanked, flat-nosed" and exuding "nauseous animal odor," and concludes their "race is not an infant, it is a degenerate." Griffith's film is guilty of nothing near so foul as that. Still, blacks and mulattoes *are* Griffith's scapegoats. The implication of *Birth*'s opening shots, beyond what the subtitle explains, is that there was hypocrisy in the traditions of those Northern white ministers whose predecessors had condoned slavery and the actions of Northern slave traders as "God's will"—whereas in later years their sons and grandsons pushed for Abolition.

But what of Southern planters who bought and kept slaves? And what are the Negroes, in these shots or elsewhere in the film, but innocent and childlike, easily led, manipulated, and deceived? The black man is either a "faithful soul," as Griffith's titles indicate, devoted to serving his white folks, or he is an arrogant, vulgar, lecherous dupe (or worse) who can be vengefully manipulated by opportunists and hypocrites. Even more telling perhaps is the villainy of mulattoes in the film—Silas Lynch and Lydia Brown, Austin Stoneman's "housekeeper" who is clearly also his mistress. Griffith, like many American whites, still had not faced the meaning of the existences of mulattoes. Who fathered them? And who mothered them? And under what circumstances? Better to make them not just scapegoats, but villains.

Griffith challenged the hypocrisy of the North and of many Abolitionists, and wanted us to feel that honorable behavior was made almost impossible for many Southern white men after the Civil War—or at least he makes one understand how some of them could feel that it was. Perhaps Griffith even saw that, by its final ride, his Clan had itself become as much committed to its own kind of vengeance as it was to the restoration of order—even a vigilante order. Nevertheless, the beginnings of wisdom do not lie in the examination of other people's wrongdoing but of one's own, and the beginning of wisdom about the South and the Civil War and its

The aftermath of the heroism of war. The Birth of a Nation.

aftermath does not lie in an examination of the hypocrisy of the North.

In Griffith's Reconstruction, the Southerner is a put-upon innocent: Ben Cameron is given the childlike epithet "little Colonel."
It is all very well to claim, as Griffith himself did on occasion, that
the historical Klan was originally formed as a vigilante movement
to restore order to a land that was impoverished, exploited, and
made lawless by Northern carpetbaggers, by their cronies the
Southern scalawags who were given a taste of power, and by their
manipulated black allies. But even that often protested position is
poor history. Allen Trealease's book *The Ku Klux Klan Conspiracy
and Southern Reconstruction* shows that, from the very beginning,
the Klan inevitably attracted bullies, thieves, rapists, and murderers,
and did not necessarily turn them away. And the "Clan" of *The
Birth of a Nation* is formed in the film specifically to frighten and
subdue superstitious blacks and presumptuous mulattoes.

Arlene Croce has called *The Birth of a Nation* "the first, the first, the most stunning and durably audacious of all American film masterpieces, and the most wonderful movie ever made." She points out that the hysteria, Griffith's own as well as that of both his detractors and his defenders, attaches to the second half of his film. In that half the director seems less confident and more defensive. The titles become long and "tensely pedantic," and the citation of select historians and other authorities to bolster a point becomes fairly constant. Then the Clan "arises with all the restraints thrown aside in the wild, oblivious surge of superstitious fears and fancies with which the film ends. A noble epic becomes no less brilliant, an opera utterly beserk. We have gone from a shot of dead soldiers at Petersburg to Lillian Gish contemplating forced marriage to a mulatto. Each is right in its own emotional scale, but the change hits you like an evasion, a personal failing, and that is what it is."

Miss Croce concludes:

> In Griffith there were the inequalities that are always confounding in artists of enormous size and uncertain weight. Futile to reason among them. Sophistication and naïveté. Pat formulations and poetry of sudden, eccentric force. *The Birth of a Nation* impossibly combines Dion Boucicault and Leo Tolstoy. Tolstoyan in its psychological acuity is the scene in the cupboard where, terrified, hiding from scalawags, Mae Marsh finds she cannot stop giggling.
>
> Mastery and tenderness of characterization, instinctive mastery of form: these were his gifts to movies. . . . The Victorian Pathos is absolute. . . . [All Griffith's films] have great performances and lyric or epic narrative designing on a scale barely conceivable in its own day, unimaginable in ours. . . . [*The Birth of a Nation's*] galvanic energy, its austerity and mad, tragic emotions are new every time. Griffith made it only fifty years after Appomattox; almost as many years since he himself had been a child submerged by what in a memorable title he called "the land's miserere"— Reconstruction. The pain it reveals is the American trauma of race. What you see in *The Birth of a Nation* is the travail of an artist whose 19th-century generosity of spirit struggles, and then fails, to deal with that trauma, and ends by succumbing to it anew.

Griffith did not see black men as wronged men, wrenched from their own culture, treated with great cruelty, and forced to hard labor. And he was puzzled when he was accused of being anti-Negro, for it seemed to him that he was not. "They were our children, whom we loved and cared for all our lives," he once said of Negroes. Precisely. Children. And he genuinely could not see the prejudice in that attitude. Griffith could not face black men as men, with the aspirations, potential, weaknesses, and capabilities of men, entitled to the dignities of men.

To whose life does the film give meaning? Taken as history, to the white Southerners' life. The life of the whole country that had not (and probably still has not) sifted the meaning of a terrible war and its causes and consequences. And above all, to its director's life. *The Birth of a Nation* justifies the life of "Roaring Jake" Griffith—not as it was, but as Griffith's never-do-well father said it was, and as Griffith himself deeply needed to believe it was.

Seven

Intolerance:
The Great Fugue

Joseph Henaberry, who played Lincoln in *The Birth of a Nation* and who later became a film director, was convinced that audiences responded so deeply to the film not only because of its characters and its plot, but because of its creative use of the film medium itself. "They felt in their inner souls," he said, "that something had really grown and developed—and this was a kind of fulfillment. . . ."

Griffith's next film, which he eventually called *Intolerance,* is apt to seem relatively more modern in theme and technique. Indeed, it was ahead of its time, and in a sense it has taken the years since for film practices and film audiences to catch up with it. It had the most modest of beginnings. Before *The Birth of a Nation* was released, Griffith had nearly completed a little picture to be called *The Mother and the Law* based on a couple of contemporary incidents, one involving a trial, the other a labor strike.

Griffith's supervisory and administrative position had changed somewhat. Harry Aitken had approached him about forming another company with a stronger creative base than Reliance-Majestic-Mutual. The proposition was that Griffith should join with his old friend, actor Mack Sennett, who was now producing Keystone comedies, and with Thomas Ince, now producing dramas, in

Triangle Company, for purposes of better prestige and distribution. Griffith and the others consented. Griffith's duties at Triangle were largely the same as they had been at Mutual. He trained directors, supervised production, suggested projects, etc., usually under the Triangle subsidiary trademark "Fine Arts." He also provided plots for a number of films, usually under the favorite of his several pseudonyms, "Granville Warwick." One of these films was an interesting Mae Marsh-Robert Harron vehicle called *Hoodoo Ann* (1916), directed by Lloyd Ingraham. The actress Bessie Love, whom Griffith discovered about this time and cast in Fine Arts films and in *Intolerance,* remembered, "Oh, that hard, hard, work. We had scarcely finished one picture when another was begun. One of Mr. Griffith's directorial staff—John O'Brien, Lloyd Ingraham, or Christy Cabanne, for instance—would rehearse the film, and Mr. Griffith would take the final run through before shooting. When he arrived, of course, the whole production came to life." Griffith later protested, however, that Fine Arts did use the title which claimed a film was "Personally Supervised by D. W. Griffith" rather freely, and often when it was simply untrue.

It was under these circumstances that Griffith came to feel *The Mother and the Law* was inadequate as a film to follow *The Birth of a Nation.* Still, its theme of intolerance grew in importance in his mind. His strong plot concerned the efforts of the "Uplifters," a group of moral reformers and prohibitionists in a small factory town. The sister of the local factory owner, an energetic woman with too little to fill her personal life, sets out to organize her friends to refine the "lower classes" and promote "laws to make people good." She ends up depriving them of their pleasures, including dancing and the local beerhall. Soon, in an effort to get more money to help support her activities in this "important" work, her brother cuts wages at his mill. This results in a strike which is cruelly put down by the local militia. The workers move to the big city nearby, where they find no work, and where hunger and the temptations of crime and prostitution become part of their daily lives. The story now centers on the Dear One (Mae Marsh) and the Boy (Bobby Harron). The Boy is framed for a crime and is wrongly accused of murder. The Dear One is deprived of their child by the Uplifters; they contend that she is incapable of raising it properly. The Boy is sentenced to be hanged. After the true culprit confesses, there is a brilliantly cross-cut, last-minute rescue of the Boy actually on the gallows.

As Griffith finally rendered this plot on the screen, it has at least two great moments. During the trial of the Boy, we learn of its progress and the verdict chiefly as the camera centers in huge close ups on the face and hands of Mae Marsh. Griffith shows us a pained and anxious smile trembling through her tears at moments, and then cuts suddenly to show us her hands, the fingers convulsively gripping the skin. Indeed, Miss Marsh's face is magnificently used in this film, and the way it evolves from youthful, eager innocence to haggard, premature age is an example of superb filmic character acting. There is another superb cut which achieves its effect by defying space. We see the Uplifters led by the industrialist's sister—the Vestal Virgins of Uplift, a subtitle calls them—in the slums, dispensing charity and moral guidance to the now destitute poor ex-workers, keeping them from drink, gambling, and prostitution. Then immediately we see the striking workers being shot down by the militia called out at the request of the industrialist.

With success of *The Birth of a Nation,* Griffith began to expand on his little follow-up film, *The Mother and the Law.* He re-shot the execution, and, with Joseph Henaberry doing research, he staged a lavish party for the factory owner and his friends to contrast with the poverty into which the workers had been thrust. Then the idea of a film that was "a protest against despotism and injustice in every form" began to possess him. He ordered his assistants to prepare for a production on a scale so lavish that it still has no equal. The first project was the Fall of Babylon. Griffith decided to reconstruct an entire culture. He had "Spec" Hall and his carpenters design and build a huge main set that was more than a mile deep. The walls

Robert Harron, moments before ascending the gallows. The modern sequence in Intolerance.

of the city were to be so wide that two horse-drawn chariots could ride on them abreast. Massive columns were topped with carved elephants. A gate that could be closed only by many men turning at two enormous turnstiles was designed and constructed by a Griffith carpenter, Huck Wortman. Joseph Henaberry remembered, "The walls of Babylon were ninety feet high. The walls were about the same height as the columns on which the elephants were erected; it is safe to estimate the overall height at one hundred and forty feet."

For a film laid in such a set (and there were others in the story almost equally lavish, but not so large) Griffith of course had to work with thousands of extras (400 on one day's shooting). To get

The grandest film set from the biggest spectacle ever. The "mile deep" Babylonian set from Intolerance.

The walls of Babylon under attack in Intolerance.

the right natural lighting, he had to limit his outdoor work to cer-
tain hours of the day, usually between 10 and 11 A.M. Wisely,
Griffith devised for this grandiose production a story which involved
princes and peasants, high priests, generals and slaves. Within
Babylon, it involved the treachery of the high priests of Bel against
King Belshazzar and their betrayal of the city to Cyrus and the
Persians. At the same time, Griffith showed an unsophisticated
Mountain Girl who had come down to the big city and fallen hope-
lessly in love with the monarch Belshazzar. It was she who learned
of the treachery of the priests and made a last minute attempt to
save the city and her king.

As a third presentation of the theme, "how hatred and intolerance have battled against love," Griffith built a story around the
massacre of the Huguenots in 1572. Again, he constructed impressive
sets of various kinds, particularly that for the French court of
Charles and his domineering mother Catherine de' Medici. He made
it clear, incidentally, that he felt that Catherine's motives were political rather than religious, and he depicted intolerance on both sides
of the conflict. Finally Griffith filmed the ministry, betrayal, and
crucifixion of Jesus, referred to as "the Nazarine." Here the presentation is briefer, more stylized, even symbolic. When Jesus, for example, performs his first miracle, transforming the water into wine at
the wedding feast, the shadow of the cross falls across his body.

All of this—scripts, shots, design of sets—Griffith kept in his
head. And when he had finished his shooting and begun his editing,
he put together a film, not four separate, self-contained stories, but
an intercutting of the four plot threads, in which the action of one
story parallels or reinforces or contrasts with that of another, in one
gigantic cinematic fugue. The intercut climaxes of the four stories
rush across the screen in a hail of images, some of them only a few
feet or a few frames long. As Iris Barry has put it, "History itself
seems to pour like a cataract across the screen."

Lillian Gish has asserted that Griffith originally intended an

The Huguenot massacre begins. From the French episode of Intolerance.

eight-hour film to be shown in two parts on two consecutive evenings, but was dissuaded from issuing such a film by exhibitors and theater men. In any case, when *Intolerance* opened after twenty months of production, it was two and a half hours long and magnificently edited. Internally, Griffith set up the pattern of dramatic rhythm in his editing that is prime evidence of his cinematic genius. The rhythm of cutting from one shot to the next, the beautiful composition of the shots themselves, the emotions of the characters and situation, and the movements of his actors within shots all reinforce each other in secret esthetic ways—but in this film there are not only recurrent motifs or subplots but the interplaying rhythm of four separate stories. A shot may be cut before its action is quite completed. Camera movement parallels and reinforces the movement in the scene. Masks on the lens and irises in or out may help effect a transition or briefly frame important details—indeed by the use of such framing devices, the size and shape of the screen is constantly made flexible according to the best demands of the drama.

Movement is unceasing. Christ toils up the side of Calvary; the Mountain Girl of Babylon races to her king to tell him of the onrush of Cyrus's armies; the Huguenot hero fights his way through the crowded, turbulent streets to reach his betrothed; the Dear One speeds by car to her husband at the prison gallows with the governor's pardon in her hand. Paul O'Dell has counted 111 shots in the five-minute murder sequence in the modern story alone.

The camera participates in this film as never before. In its most famous shot, at the opening of the feast of Belshazzar, Griffith (before the days of the flexible camera crane) began a quarter of a mile from the end of the great court, a set which was itself over a mile deep. He moved gradually forward and down, over the heads of extras and dancing girls, to enter into the action of the city and its people. The high tower which enabled Griffith to gain this effect resembled one of the siege towers that he used so effectively in his battle scenes. It was 140 feet high and was mounted on six sets of railroad tracks. It had an inside elevator that carried the director and crew to the top and was manipulated on its tracks by twenty-five men.

When we first see the French court, it appears as an elaborate expanse in an extreme long-shot. Then the camera enters the room and moves, approximately at eye level, into the action almost as a participant. It moves among the players until we see King Charles on his throne. Then it pans to the right and ultimately rests on the prince and heir to the throne whose effeteness and decadence are obvious. Griffith had his carpenters build a ceiling on the set—a then unheard of and still rare practice—and, by showing it to us at certain moments, he gained a strong ironic effect of elegance and confinement.

The orgy has begun. From Intolerance.

A production sketch for one of the interior sets for Intolerance. The atmosphere of orgy lay largely in the imagination of the sketch artist, although later in New York Joseph Henaberry did shoot, at the distributors' insistance, some semi-nude females which were intercut into the film's orgy sequence.

In the modern story, there is an extreme long-shot of the industrialist in his office where he is lord of *his* domain; it tells us in itself more about him than action might tell us, particularly if we relate the scene to that of Charles's court, as Griffith invites us to.

Bitzer had staggering problems in photographing this film—simply maintaining continuity of lighting from one shot to the next was a large one—but he met them all. He used an assistant for the first time, Karl Brown, who later photographed the celebrated *Covered Wagon*. He also used four camera simultaneously on some of the mass battle sequences.

Intolerance, the biggest film ever made, opened at the Liberty Theatre in New York on September 5, 1916. For four months, it was a success, even outgrossing *The Birth of a Nation*. Then, attendance suddenly began to fall off, and the picture was withdrawn after another month. In other cities, the same pattern was repeated: an initial success, followed by a quick decline. Griffith had said anxiously before its opening that "*Intolerance* must succeed": it failed, and the failure meant enormous financial failure for Griffith and the Wark Producing Company, which he had formed to produce and distribute it. Initially he had found backers (mostly bankers) only too happy to help him after the success of *The Birth of a Nation,* but, as production became more lavish and costs mounted, these men complained loudly. Griffith, in pique, took the financial reins away from them and assumed the burden himself. *Intolerance* thus became the money failure from which he never really recovered.

It has been suggested that the techniques Griffith used in the film were simply too much for the audiences of the time, and that they found *Intolerance* confusing. It is true that it took until the 1960s for directors and film editors to re-introduce the sustained jump-cutting of such brief lengths of film. It was suggested at the time that Griffith had—just this once—used battle scenes somewhat for their own sake, for the thrills and spectacle involved, and, at any rate, had not sufficiently aroused audience sympathy for Babylon.

Perhaps audiences did not like the idea that Babylon *did* lose and that the Huguenots *were* massacred. But as Edward Wagenknecht has remarked, no one has ever really explained the public failure of *Intolerance*.

Today, we are apt to be bothered by sentimental names like the little Dear One and Princess Beloved, and by some of the moralistic titles—written by Anita Loos, incidentally. (Griffith's initial intention had been to use *no* subtitles until he was persuaded by Miss Loos that audiences would need them.) Yet we see *Intolerance* as Griffith's greatest film of all, greatest and most modern and durable in theme, outlook, and technique. The original tints are gone in most prints of *Intolerance* that survive* and, indeed, no known prints are absolutely complete. But even projected in a 16 mm print on a small screen, *Intolerance* is still an overwhelming cinematic experience.

Intolerance's structure had a curious effect on that of several subsequent Biblical epics. Griffith juxtaposed a modern tale, a bible story, and an ancient spectacle. The practice continued throughout the silent era: Cecil B. De Mille framed *The Ten Commandments* (first version, 1923) with a modern parable, as Michael Curtiz did his stunning *Noah's Ark* (1929); both films thus echoed in miniature the structural and thematic premise of *Intolerance*.

Intolerance was widely shown in Russia and was very influential among the great Russian directors, Sergei Eisenstein and V. Pudovkin. In some versions it was re-edited and re-titled so that the Babylonian story became a warning against church rule, the medieval story described the collaboration of church and state, and the modern story showed the oppressive evils of capitalism. Indeed, even Russian filmmakers who knew the original version were surprised to learn that Griffith was not a communist, though Griffith, an apolitical man, was too interested, surely, in the individual and the individual conscience to have become one. All in all, we are apt to fully understand Lillian Gish's remark that she thinks of

---

* Tints have been more or less successfully restored in the prints now available from at least two distributors, however.

Intolerance when she remembers Griffith's hopeful words, "We have gone beyond Babel, beyond words. We have found a universal language, a power that can make men brothers and end war forever. Remember that! Remember that when you stand in front of the camera!"

Eight

Hearts of the World
and
True Heart Susie

Intolerance opened to competition from several spectacle films, most of them also shown at advanced prices in large, "legitimate" theaters and usually inspired by the example Griffith had set. Thomas W. Dixon himself came up with a war spectacle, *The Fall of a Nation.* Thomas H. Ince offered *Civilization* on German militarism. William Fox cast the swimmer Annette Kellermann in *A Daughter of the Gods.* Cecil B. De Mille offered a fictional version of Joan of Arc in *Joan the Woman,* with the opera star Geraldine Farrar. There were films of *Oliver Twist, Ramona, King Lear,* and *Romeo and Juliet.* Less pretentiously, there was a burlesque of *Carmen* with Charlie Chaplain.

One of the most revealing documents about D. W. Griffith and his working methods—indeed probably one of the most revealing about any American artist—is Karl Brown's *Adventures with D. W. Griffith.* Brown in his teens began as an assistant to Billy Bitzer with Griffith at Reliance-Majestic-Mutual. (Bitzer had joined Griffith only reluctantly, by the way, at first feeling, typically, that the move from the security of Biograph was a foolish one.) Brown saw that Griffith set up competitive rivalries among the many assistants, craftsmen, and technicians who worked for him, but succeeded in getting the best out of each and discouraged few.

One of Griffith's extras on *The Birth of a Nation,* who had also served as an assistant in staging some of the crowd scenes, was a Vienna-born actor named Eric von Stroheim. Von Stroheim served in something like the same capacity on *Intolerance.* He played a Pharisee in the New Testament sequences, he assisted Griffith throughout the film, and he performed a similar function for Griffith's next film. He learned his directing craft well, and, when his own chance came, von Stroheim went on to make such outstanding films as *Foolish Wives, The Wedding March, The Merry Widow,* and *Greed.* Those pictures show a very different sensibility from Griffith's and a very different viewpoint on men and their ways, and they are therefore a tribute to the universality of Griffith's discoveries about film technique. William K. Everson has put it that "while Stroheim learned the *mechanics* of the movies from Griffith, he learned nothing from him philosophically. The *types* of stories they told were antipathetic, and so was the *way* they told them. Griffith liked to find beauty amid squalor and despair . . . , Stroheim preferred to find ugliness and depravity amid luxury and elegance. . . . For Griffith the *means* were often as important as the story itself—his films had elaborate friezes of cross-cutting, panel shots, vignettes, cutbacks, and other technical . . . devices to heighten a theme's excitement and power. To Stroheim only story mattered. . . ."

Incidentally, another subsequently famous director who started with Griffith was Tod Browning, later known particularly for his horror classics. He played a crook in the modern story in *Intolerance.*

Griffith used Lillian Gish sparingly in *Intolerance* as the "Eternal Mother," a recurring motif between sequences of the film, in a shot of a mother rocking her child, with the title, "out of the cradle endlessly rocking," from Walt Whitman's poem by the same name. In the public mind, to be sure, Miss Gish was a star after *The Birth of a Nation,* if she had not already been one before that. But in the early prints of that film, there were no credits for the actors, although the printed programs that went with showings gave a list of their names.

It was an axiom in the business by this time that D. W. Griffith was a star-maker, and that any actor who worked for him would get better treatment from other studios. As we know, he himself came quite reluctantly to accept and use the "star system" for its attractiveness at the box office. After *Judith of Bethulia,* Blanche Sweet had received an enticing offer from the company headed by Jesse Lasky, Cecil B. De Mille, and Samuel Goldfish (later Goldwyn).

They came to my house in Hollywood and offered me a wonderful financial deal. . . . I went to Mr. Griffith and told him of the offer, hoping he'd counter with an offer of his own, for I definitely would have preferred staying with him. Instead, he told me he thought I'd learned everything I could from him, and that it would probably be better if I tried my own wings, somewhere else. So I signed with Lasky.

Mae Marsh's experience was similar. Her tributes to Griffith and his methods were always high.

He was an inspiration to all who worked for him. . . . Often his stories were written as rehearsals took form. With his quick eye, the rehearsals often furnished him with inspiration he would not have gained from a shooting-script. His energy was astounding. . . . With this energy I remember best his infinite patience. . . . He had the patience to make us succeed. He never despaired, no matter how backward we might be. . . . We always had the wonderful feeling he was intensely loyal to us all. . . . He never lorded it over his players. . . . He would say, "You understand this situation. Now let us see what you would do with it."

In this way he drew out the best in his players, and by seeming to depend on them to stand upon their own feet, maintained an enthusiasm among them—a sort of family spirit—that I have never seen equalled in any other studio. He was big enough not to be small about receiving suggestions, but for every idea we gave him, he returned us a hundred.

When she was about to leave him to work for Goldwyn, Griffith said to Mae Marsh, in effect, "This is your chance to make enough money to keep you for the rest of your life. Take it, and when you have the money come back to me and we'll start again where we left off." She compared his methods to the improvisational approach of the *Commedia dell'Arte,* and she concluded that by the time rehearsing was over, Griffith knew the running length of his finished film.

Dorothy Gish has remarked on the care of those rehearsals that, "by the time a photoplay went into actual production, an actor was thoroughly familiar with his own part, as well as the tempo, approach, and reactions of all the other actors." But the director was not above using whatever method he thought would work best with his actors, even if it was temporarily unpleasant. We have noted his clashes with his first big star, Mary Pickford. During the filming of *The Birth of a Nation,* Griffith had placed a promising (and soon to be famous) young actor named Wallace Reid on standby for Henry B. Walthall, whose kidney ailment might have prevented him from playing the Little Colonel. Reid's wife remembered that

just as he was about to start work, word came that Walthall had recovered sufficiently to assume the role. Griffith tried to assuage Wally's disappointment by telling him he had him in mind for another role in the picture, one which would undoubtedly make him star material. When Wally found out what Griffith had in mind was the small but dramatic bit of Jeff, the blacksmith, he was incensed to the point of mayhem—a reaction the wily Mr. Griffith had counted on. It worked—and how! Every poor guy Wally threw out of that blacksmith shop in his scene was D. W. Griffith.

Norma Talmadge was already an established star when she and her sister Constance joined Fine Arts-Triangle in late 1915. Griffith chose Constance for the Mountain Girl in *Intolerance,* a part which required the kind of humor which Miss Talmadge could project. "Constance [like Dorothy Gish] was not awed by Griffith," her mother remembered,

and whenever she saw him, on the lot or off, hailed him and talked to him. Part of Constance's value to Mr. Griffith lay in the fact that she amused him, just as she had amused Mr. Ince and the others back in the Vitagraph days. . . . She made him laugh largely because of her absolute disregard of his importance, in contrast to the awe and respect and head-bowing accorded him by all the others. They rarely approached him if they could help it, save on matters of the utmost importance, while Constance, to Norma's frequent horror, would rush up to him with everything, anything, be it trivial or be it great. After a while they became such good friends—this leggy girl and the great man—that he would often send for her when he had a few spare moments and say: "Just sent for you, Constance, because I want to laugh."

"Well, here I am, Your Majesty may begin at once," was her stock reply. She would make a salaam of mock humility, and the very sight of her seemed to set him up immediately. . . .

When Griffith told her she would play the Mountain Girl, Constance pretended she was hurt and said she must have looked pretty dowdy to him for him to have chosen that part for her. But then, her mother said, "she was so elated, so proud and pleased and excited, that she threw both arms about him in a strangling grip and simply hugged and hugged him! They had a long talk then, Mr. Griffith and this funny girl, and she promised him, with tears in her laughing eyes that she would do her very, very best, and would study every day and practice every angle of her part."

If *Intolerance* was a financial failure for Griffith, a failure from which his professional career never really recovered, it was in no sense a personal one. Eileen Bowser has commented that now he was

hailed as the Shakespeare of the screen and he walked with the great of his time, the wealthy and the socially prominent. Although he knew he had poured his heart into *The Birth of a Nation* and *Intolerance,* he must have been a bit bewildered to have achieved such success in the medium he had originally despised. His was an intuitive genius and fame made him self-conscious. His deliberate striving for artistic excellence or for popularity in his later films led him at times to descend into mannerism. The financial failure of *Intolerance* made him aware of the need to cater to popular taste, yet he was never sure of what popular taste was. No amount of success quite gave him full confidence in his powers, and failure, when it did arrive, was what he had been half-expecting all the time. His written and spoken words became pompous, at times cynical.

The film industry was changing, as we know, largely because of what Griffith had shown that film could do. Small enterprise was becoming corporate endeavor, with the successful producer taking a more direct part in esthetic matters. Make-up, for example, became a matter for a studio department to attend to, not something the actor did for himself, and, increasingly, sets were not made up and executed by carpenters in collaboration with directors, but conceived by artistic directors and production designers.

Griffith did not have an orderly personal life to fall back on. He was, for better or worse, married to his job. He and Linda Arvidson had inevitably separated in 1911, two years before the end of his Biograph days, Griffith to follow the dictates of his cinematic muse, and she at first to follow her acting career—indeed, she had been associated as a leading player with that very Kinemacolor Company which had sought to film *The Clansman.* I do not mean to imply in this, however, that Griffith was celibate. Billy Bitzer has told of how Linda Griffith broke up his romance with Biograph actress Dorothy West and there were undoubtedly others. The fact that rumors and legends of Griffith's liaisons with certain of his leading actresses have been frequently denied does not convince one that they were all untrue. But if Miriam Cooper's experience was typical, his advances to women must have been sometimes awkward and compulsive. Again according to Miriam Cooper, however, the actors at Biograph and Majestic generally treated Lillian Gish as "Griffith's girl."

On March 17, 1917, Griffith set sail for London. He was to attend the opening of *Intolerance* and to discuss an offer from the British Government to make a propaganda film for the war effort. Very much in the background was the fact that the United States seemed about to enter the World War. Also, there was the success of two films: Ince's *Civilization,* which was anti-war and also anti-German, and *The Battle Cry of Peace,* from J. Stuart Blackton, which was pro-war and anti-German. The Triangle company was in artistic and financial trouble, and, on the day that he sailed, Griffith announced that he was severing his ties with Triangle Films. He and his operation would join Artcraft, the company of Adolph Zukor, which now produced for Famous Player-Lasky and later became Paramount Pictures—the company which had been successfully hiring away Triangle's directors and stars.

In London, Griffith was impressively welcomed. He became a devoted Anglophile and a friend of the publisher, Lord Beaverbrook. He accepted the British Government's offer and set out for France, where he toured the battlefields and the muddy trenches, and saw at first hand the holocaust and the suffering of the soldiers and the civilians. He determined to convey these grim and terrible facts of war to Americans. He shot footage on the battlefields, often actually under fire, in France. In New York he had acquired some battle footage from a German national, a Captain Kleinschmidt. But he shot most of his film in California. He called it *Hearts of the World*.

"Viewed as drama, the war is disappointing," Griffith said. Perhaps he knew that any war is. He chose to tell it as "the story of a village, an old fashioned play with a new fashioned theme," the effects of the war on a French town and its people. The men go to war. Then the war comes to the village, it is captured, occupied, its people made to work for the enemy. From one point of view, Griffith had reworked plot motifs of *The Birth of a Nation*. But he

DAVID LLOYD GEORGE
AND D.W.GRIFFITH.
64.G

David Lloyd George greets D. W. Griffith in London in 1917. A some-
what retouched and much used publicity photo.

made an exceptional film nevertheless. Individual shots are gorgeous, one after another. Even when they portray violence or terror, they are apt to be individually beautiful, and the beauty of the individual frames heightens the violence.

Lillian Gish's performance is exceptional. She is lovely, fragile, touching, restrained. The scene where she wanders in a daze through the scarred landscape, carefully holding her unused wedding dress, is unforgettable. It walks a narrow line of genuine pathos between melodramatic absurdity on the one hand and bathos on the other. Dorothy Gish, in a brunette wig, is delightful in a saucy, comic interpretation, which solidified the characterization on which she built her subsequent career. Indeed, the pacing of this film and the balancing of comedy and melodrama are exceptional, and the details are carefully executed. Incidentally, Dorothy Gish, in a contemporary interview, attributed the basis of her characterization to an English girl—and to Griffith. "Mr. Griffith saw her on the Strand one day, freshness, wig-wag walk and all. He followed her for hours— or, rather, we did. I thought he was dreadful to make me play her. I didn't like her, I thought she was crazy. But Mr. Griffith insisted, and I cried. He insisted some more—and I did. I'm glad now."

Griffith was bold on occasion in *Hearts of the World*. He set a sentimental love-rejection scene, with comic undertones, in the bright sunlight, and made it work. His battles, burnings, and sacking are real. Griffith's Germans are not quite real, however. They are the heavies and villains, so much so that we do not quite grasp their deeds as the believable cruelties of human beings. It is interesting that in the early British prints of this film, their treatment was somewhat softer. There is a scene in which the fragile Miss Gish is forced to work in the fields and beaten by a German soldier when she does not fill her quota. In the British prints, another soldier intervenes, lets her go, and remarks in a subtitle that *all* Germans are not so heartless. Indeed, *Hearts of the World* was shown in several versions. Before Griffith began shooting, the United States had entered the war—the ship that took G. W. Bitzer, Robert Harron, and

Robert Harron and a very young Ben Alexander in Hearts of the World.

Dorothy Gish to England also carried General Pershing. In the American version, there are some rather self-gratulatory concluding scenes which strongly imply that the arrival of the Yanks saved the day for everyone. The picture was a firm financial success, and a quick one. However, the armistice that ended the war was imminent when it was released in April 1918. Subsequently, therefore, *Hearts of the World* was cut still another time to fit the peace. And then Zukor wanted, and eventually got, a shorter version for Artcraft distribution.

While he was in Europe, Griffith wired his California associates to save all out-takes and discarded scenes from *Intolerance*. He had in mind an effort to save some of his losses on that film. With re-editing, and newly-shot footage, and a new happy ending for his Mountain Girl tacked on (she had originally been killed by an ar-

A theater lobby poster for Hearts of the World *speaks for itself.*

row in the final battle), he salvaged a spectacular *The Fall of Baby-lon* from *Intolerance,* and he opened it in New York with live spec-tacle and dance on stage supplementing the action of the film during the orgy sequence. Then he restored *The Mother and the Law* and played it too as a separate film, a film which Antony Slide in *The Films of D. W. Griffith* calls one of the master's best. When se-quences for *The Mother and the Law* were extracted, Griffith and his cutters went back to the original negative of *Intolerance* itself, and re-cut from it. This is still another reason why accurate and complete prints of that great film are hard, not to say impossible, to come by today.

By late 1918, Griffith was back in California and had set to work for Paramount-Artcraft and Adolph Zukor. He completed *Hearts of the World* there. He supervised a new series of comedies for Dorothy Gish. (Her directors, incidentally, between 1914 and 1920, included William Christy Cabanne, Donald Crisp, Paul Powell, George Seigmann, Elmer Clifton—and, for *Remodeling Her Hus-band* in 1920, Lillian Gish.) And he used her sister Lillian and Robert Harron in some rather modest films of his own. *The Great Love,* with a story laid in London during the war, used some footage Griffith had made there, chiefly of certain figures in London politics and society who had pursued him and entertained him during his stay. There are no known surviving prints of *The Great Love* today. *A Romance of Happy Valley* is a small and somewhat brief rural melodrama for which Griffith undoubtedly was drawing on the scenes of his own early boyhood in Kentucky. He added some melo-dramatic twists to the old tale of the country boy who makes a for-tune in the city and comes home to distribute his bounty. Lillian Gish's performance in this film seems surprisingly mannered and unreal, as though she did not feel her character or situation.

The Greatest Thing in Life was another war story. All prints of it, too, seem to have been lost, but Lillian Gish remembers it as exceptional, and some observers have seen it as an answer to the accusations of prejudice leveled at Griffith after *The Birth of a*

Griffith with Mrs. Buller, Lady Diana Manners, Elizabeth Asquith, and the Duchess of Beaufors. Footage shot in London during work on Hearts of the World *was used in* The Great Love.

Nation. It was at any rate a bold film. Harron is an intolerant snob, a prejudiced Southern officer whose attitudes are broken down in the stress of battle. He finds himself in the same shell hole as a Negro private. The black man rescues Harron when he is hit, but is himself fatally wounded. As he lies dying, the Negro dazedly calls for his mother. The white officer responds by pretending to be the mother and kisses the private on the lips. For *The Girl Who Stayed at Home,* Griffith again used footage shot in Europe, this time battle footage. Carol Dempster (who had danced in *Intolerance*) was his heroine, and a young actor named Richard Barthelmess his hero.

True Heart Susie, released in June of 1919, is the little master-piece of the Artcraft series. For it, Griffith returned to a fragile and sentimental rural tale, and made his best such film, with appropriately simple technique in camera movement and editing. He also

Lillian Gish in The Greatest Thing in Life.

returned to one of his favorite authors, Charles Dickens. But somewhat obliquely so, for the plot of this film, which has to do with a
girl too innocent and too forthright to scheme at getting the husband she wants, is a distillation of elements from *David Copperfield*
and *Great Expectations*. Kevin Brownlow has confirmed that
"D. W. Griffith has been called 'the Shakespeare of the Screen' but
has more in common with Charles Dickens. The use of melodrama
amid settings of complete reality, the exaggerated yet still truthful
characters, the fascination with detail, the accuracy of dress and be-

Lillian Gish, again. True Heart Susie.

havior, the sentimentality, the attitude toward religion, the outrage over social justice, are all points which their works have in common." However, Brownlow continues, for all the Dickensian melodrama, the memorable moments in Griffith's films are those which are handled with most subtlety and delicacy, and these come chiefly from the heartbreaking poignancy that Griffith got from his actresses. In *True Heart Susie,* Lillian Gish redeems her performance in *A Romance of Happy Valley.* Eileen Bowser says of her in this role that she rises "above the cloying sweetness of the role." She explains that "her skillful acting makes this sentimental story genuinely moving, however, and as the naive but faithful Susie, she grows in stature from a funny, happy adolescent to a dignified woman. Only at the end is her characterization marred when in response to Harron's proposal, she reverts to the cuteness of adolescence."

For his final Artcraft release, *Scarlet Days,* Griffith returned to the Western film for the first time since his Biograph days, and for the last time. His story (initially supplied by S. E. V. Taylor) is set in California in 1875, and is loosely based on the exploits of the Mexican bandit-hero, Joaquin Murietta. Griffith again cast Richard Barthelmess and Carol Dempster as his leads. Eileen Bowser comments that the dance-hall girls in this film are depicted with a down-to-earth realism quite unusual for the movies, except in the remarkably realistic westerns that William S. Hart was making for Thomas Ince at the time. *Scarlet Days* like several other of the Artcraft films shows carelessness and haste. Shots within scenes are carelessly matched, in decor, in costume, in make-up—time and again an actor's movement in a medium shot (a turn left of the head, a cigarette to the mouth) will be repeated in the following close up. The composition of individual shots also seems sometimes hasty and careless, and they do not show Griffith's superb painter's eye. It is as though Griffith had shot hastily and not supervised a quick editing.

In *The Parade's Gone By* Kevin Brownlow comments that, having shown the effectiveness of camera angle and close-ups and established the primacy of rhythm in film editing, Griffith became almost indifferent to the details of their execution. He would do his long-shots on one occasion, his close-ups on another. An actor's pace of movement, even the details of his "business" and his state of dress, might not quite match from one shot to the next. Sometimes sets and backgrounds mismatched as well. As usual, the intuitive will, in which lay Griffith's genius, simply over-rode the facts. Nevertheless, in an association of a year and a half with Artcraft, Griffith had directed *Hearts of the World* and *True Heart Susie*. Before he left, he was already at work on another of his most memorable films, *Broken Blossoms*.

$\mathcal{N}ine$

Broken Blossoms
and
Way Down East

During November of 1918—even before he had undertaken *The Girl Who Stayed at Home* with Barthelmess and Dempster—Griffith began preliminary work on a movie to be based on a short story called "The Chink and the Child." The tale came from a collection by Thomas Burke called *Limehouse Nights,* short stories laid in the Chinese district of London. The book had been brought to Griffith's attention by Douglas Fairbanks and Mary Pickford who felt the director could make a wonderful film out of it. Griffith approached the project in the spirit of making another "programmer," a pot-boiler, but as he worked on it, he decided to make it one of his "big" pictures, one of his "specials," and lavished much care on it.

It was an unlikely choice for an important Griffith picture. A relatively brief, sentimental tale, with no spectacle needed in the telling and no last minute chase and rescue, *Broken Blossoms* (as it came to be called) told of an idealistic young Chinese named Cheng, who came to London during World War I to teach the Western white man of the peace and inner tranquility of the Buddha. There he was quickly disillusioned. It also concerned a sadistic, small-time boxer, Battling Burrows, and his unwanted, twelve-year-old daugh-

The waterfront set for Broken Blossoms. *Lillian Gish is to the right of the standing pipe-smoker.*

ter, Lucy, whom he beat regularly whenever he was frustrated or drunk. Indeed, any more detailed account of the tale will make it seem even less likely to become a film poem and a film tragedy, but that is what Griffith made of it.

Cheng discovered Lucy, after one particularly brutal beating, crawling, half-crazed, through the murky Limehouse streets. He took her home, cleaned her wounds and dressed her in silk robes and put her as a kind of play-princess on a couch which he treated as her throne, with a doll in her arms. A crony of Burrows had seen Cheng take the girl to his room, and the boxer, convinced there is something "onnatural" going on (as he put it), broke into Cheng's rooms and dragged the child off. Back at Burrows rooms, she broke away and in fright locked herself in a closet. Burrows, enraged, broke the door down and beat the terrified child to death. Cheng entered, killed Burrows, took the body of the "broken blossom" to his room, and, before a small alter, put a knife through his heart.

Griffith decided that such a tale needed a special telling. To gain absolute atmospheric control over every frame of his film, he built his sets entirely indoors and used with care only artificial light. Much of the photography is in a soft focus, and it is the work not only of Bitzer, but also—for close-ups and "special effects"—of Hendrick Sartov. A former portrait photographer whose work Lillian Gish had admired greatly, he had been used for some of her added close-ups in *Hearts of the World*. Griffith also carefully used tinted film, differently colored from scene to scene—even from shot

Lillian Gish in Broken Blossoms.

to shot. Further, he hand-tinted some scenes with additional colors. *Broken Blossoms,* in its studio-controlled atmosphere, in its scaling down of emotion, and in its theme, marked a distinct stage in American movies. In his use of atmospheric studio sets, where design, proportion, and lighting could be strictly controlled from shot to shot, Griffith may have been influenced by certain Danish productions of the time. In any case, his film had a sizable influence on production methods in Germany as well as at home. Ironically, he had originally hoped to shoot *Broken Blossoms* in London in its actual locales.

Lillian Gish was at first understandably reluctant to play a part originally conceived for a twelve-year-old child, but her performance is exceptional. The terror in her final scenes provides one of the great examples of pure pantomime in American silent films. If a sound-track of her screams had been included, the effect would have become bathetic and ludicrous; when the inner ear of the viewer provides her screams from what he sees, the effect is harrowing.

As usual, Griffith rehearsed his actors carefully, soliciting suggestions from everyone and apparently considering them all. When he started to shoot, the director blocked his scenes in long-shot, mid-shot, and close-up. The atmosphere was relaxed, with Griffith coaching quietly but enthusiastically from beside the camera. If anything went wrong during a shot, the director would abruptly change the subject of his discourse, often to jolt the actors out of "acting." Griffith sensed the moment things went wrong "internally" for his actors, when they were reaching for, or had lost, the proper motivation or emotion. He would sometimes speak their lines for them and jolt them back into character and situation—"like an experienced jockey letting a horse feel the touch of his hand on the rein," one associate put it. Big emotional scenes were carefully and still less casually approached. "Working up" scenes were shot for several days before. When the day came, the studio was quiet. Griffith rested for an hour. Then he began to coach the player, and gave always in direct ratio to the player's response. When the closet scene to *Broken*

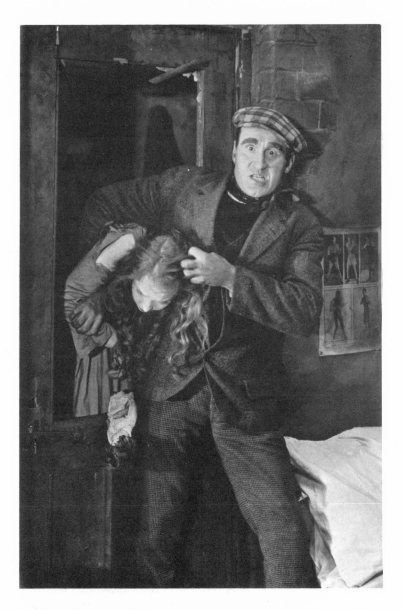

Donald Crisp and Lillian Gish after the harrowing "closet scene."

Blossoms was shot, Lillian Gish's screams and Griffith's shouts attracted such crowds outside the studio that it took the entire staff
to hold them out.

Miss Gish's performance in this film is all curves, it has been
said, and Richard Barthelmess's, as Cheng, is its perfect complement,
all angles. Essentially *Broken Blossoms* is a tale of three frightened
people. Miss Gish perceived this for herself, and Barthelmess shows
us the fear under Cheng's self-effacing calm. Donald Crisp's performance is all effective cruelty and brutality, but it may strike us
as overdone, because he did not grasp, or did not let us glimpse, the
hidden fear that a brute such as Burrows masks with arrogance and
violence.

For Griffith himself, however, the range between *Intolerance*
and *Broken Blossoms* is the range of a major artist.

When he took his film to Adolph Zukor the producer was irate.
Griffith had brought him a picture like this, and wanted *money* for
making it? A picture in which everybody *dies*. Nobody will go to
see it! You may as well put your hand in my pocket and *steal* my
money. Griffith stalked out of Zukor's office. In a few days, he returned with $250,000, which he threw on the producer's desk. Here
is your money back, he said. Sign the film over to me and give me
back my negative and my print. Griffith had other plans for his
movie now. He opened it with fanfare in New York in a "legitimate" house, the George M. Cohan Theatre, at the then unheard of
price of $3.00 a ticket. He augmented its poetic atmosphere with a
special use of colored lights thrown at the screen from behind. (The
idea came by accident. He was rehearsing a dance by Carol
Dempster that was to open the program, running the film at the
same time. Miss Dempster's lighting hit the movie screen. Griffith
was struck with the effect and decided to use it.)

The film was a success with both critics and public, and, as we
have seen, with Griffith's fellow filmmakers, here and abroad. Indeed, the reviewers were more lavish with their praise than they had
been for *The Birth of a Nation* and *Intolerance*. One declared that

it was "an eloquent and decisive flight beyond the speaking stage" and another that in *Broken Blossoms* Griffith had achieved something in pictorial drama that was quite beyond the power of the written word. On the basis of such a success (and perhaps also in retaliation against Zukor and the growing "studio system"), Griffith made some inflated public pronouncements. His next picture would be the world's greatest—seventy-two reels long. He planned to construct his own theater, "The Griffith," and then a chain of theaters across the country that would show only his pictures. He gave advice and criticism to the film industry in general, commercial as well as artistic advice, not confined to films. He attacked the income tax as weighing more heavily on the poor and the creative than on the rich. And so forth. These seem oddly like the boosts and pronouncements of a man enjoying his fame but somehow unsure of himself and of the nature and the limits of his own talents, and perhaps of a man still unconvinced of the worthiness of his real achievements. Intuition creates, creates often against expectation but it does not award confidence in the creation.

Broken Blossoms was successfully "road shown" at advanced prices in major cities. For its distribution, Griffith turned the film over to the newly formed United Artists, a company in which he was a partner.

United Artists was founded in January 1919 by four leading film artists who felt that the growth of big production companies, and of realignments within the growing film "industry," might limit both their potential earnings and their future careers. In addition to Griffith, they were Douglas Fairbanks (Griffith had paid him little attention when the actor joined Triangle a few years before, but his films, featuring a combination of acting, acrobatics, and boyish American optimism, had made him a leading player); Mary Pickford, now married to Fairbanks; and Charlie Chaplin, often called the screen's great comic artist since he joined Mack Sennett's Keystone company in 1914. At the time, Fairbanks was free to provide pictures for the new company, but Miss Pickford and Chaplin were still under contract to First National. Griffith himself still owed pictures to Zukor at Artcraft, and to raise money for the films he wanted to do for United Artists, he signed a contract for three pictures to be delivered to First National. The effort was for independence. As a part of that effort, Griffith left Hollywood and its pressures. He bought a huge house and grounds on a point of land outside Mamaroneck on Long Island Sound, New York, and began staffing it and converting it into his own film studio. He moved his company in and started production on the films for First National. Expenses were vast. By 1920, in an effort to cope with the outlay, the director formed a public company, the D. W. Griffith Corporation, with himself as a salaried employee. Griffith had rid himself of movie industry control, but to raise money he soon tied himself to investment bankers instead.

The First National films were hastily made pot-boilers, and more than one critic and film historian has suspected that they were largely made by assistants and not by the master. The first, *The Greatest Question,* was another tale of rural America with Lillian Gish and Robert Harron. It was largely completed in California before Griffith's departure for Mamaroneck. At one point during rehearsals for that film Griffith took over the role of the mother and, turning his hawk-like face heavenward, cried out, "My son, my son, can you hear me there in heaven? Say that you hear me—speak to me!" The director was quite pleased with himself, and the younger members of the cast were spellbound. But one of the older hands present knew that Griffith's performance had been pure ham and revealed it through a slight twinkle in her eye. Catching sight of this, Griffith immediately shrugged his shoulders sheepishly and sat down with "Well, something like that."

When he had finished *The Greatest Question,* Griffith set out for the Caribbean to film two tales laid in the never-never-land of the South Seas of popular literary convention. *The Idol Dancer* has respectable performances by Richard Barthelmess and others, but the composition of its shots shows nothing of Griffith's painter's eye, its editing is poor, and its over-all conception is rather slip-shod. *The Love Flower,* with Barthelmess and Carol Dempster, seems to have pleased at least the director. He shot extra footage of his heroine on his return to Mamaroneck, bought the film away from First National, and arranged for United Artists distribution. He also gave it a special preview before a convention of the American Newspaper Publishers Association, and before the screening delivered one of the many speeches on freedom of the screen he had given since *The Birth of a Nation* first appeared. The reasons for Griffith's special interest in *The Love Flower* seem obscure to us today, unless we infer his growing interest in grooming Miss Dempster for stardom obscured his perspective on the project itself.

Back at home, *The Idol Dancer* and *The Love Flower* gained wide publicity while in production. Griffith had left New York in November of 1919 for Fort Lauderdale, where he did some preliminary shooting. On December 10, he and his company, along with the mayor of Lauderdale and his staff, boarded a yacht called the *Grey Duck,* headed for Nassau, a trip of about twelve hours. They were not heard from for three days. Newspaper headlines proclaimed that the great American director, his stars, a prominent Florida mayor, and his staff were all missing and feared lost at sea. The Navy and Coast Guard were called into a search that included airplanes and private ships as well. When the *Grey Duck* was finally discovered, Griffith explained that the ship had simply put in on the lee side of Whale Key to avoid a threatened storm. Many suspected a publicity stunt, but Griffith's anxious associates in New York sincerely doubted it. In any case, *The Greatest Question* was playing in New York at the time. Its titles did include some vague talk of spiritualism and it was advertised with a line about communicating with the dead.

Production at Mamaroneck continued. Chet Withey directed *Romance,* and it lost money for United Artists. Lillian Gish directed her sister Dorothy in *Remodeling Her Husband.* The film was a success, but, like Dorothy Gish's other films, it was made for Para-

Griffith greeted by Kate Bruce after apparently being lost at sea in 1919.

mount, Zukor's company. A planned series of Bobby Harron pro-
grammers had to be abandoned when the young actor suddenly
shot himself in the summer of 1920 before the first of them, *Coin-
cidence,* was completed. There was never a great call for optimism
in the years at Mamaroneck. Griffith's secretary, Agnes Weiner,
might announce on a Friday that everyone would have to be laid
off, beginning the following week. Griffith would then single out
certain players and take them aside to say "I didn't mean you—I
want you back on Monday." He may have kept his overhead down
this way, but his general carelessness with money, and his personal

generosity to his associates, their families, his own family, and others, continued.

Griffith then bought a curious property, an old stage melodrama about an unwed mother called *Way Down East*. He paid a lot for it by the standards of the time, $165,000, over twice the total production cost of *The Birth of a Nation*. For the first time in his career, he hired someone to prepare a shooting script, a playwright named Antony Paul Kelly. As Lillian Gish puts it in her autobiography, when Mr. Griffith's associates heard that he had bought *Way Down East,* they all wondered if he had lost his mind. The play may have posed important social problems, but it did so in a pretty old fashioned way. Griffith set about to breathe new life into old bones. Happily perhaps, he paid Kelly off for his script but soon began to

Griffith directs Martha Perkins, Richard Barthelmess, Lillian Gish, Burr McIntosh, and Lowell Sherman in Way Down East.

A lobby still for Way Down East.

devise one of his own in collaboration with his actors during rehearsals.

The result does not reflect its stage origins. It is visual, and it moves. Griffith expanded on the beginning of the story to establish the background of his characters. And he expanded on the ending to stage an elaborate rescue of the heroine from an ice floe as she is about to be washed over a waterfall. Anna, a simple country girl from way down east in Maine, is tricked into a fake marriage by a big city playboy. When she becomes pregnant, he reveals the truth and abandons her. She bears the child. It dies. Alone, she finds work on a farm. David, the farmer's son (Richard Barthelmess), falls in love with Anna. The playboy, however, owns the next farm, and eventually Anna's secret is revealed. In the tradition of such melodrama, her father turns her out—straight into a blizzard. She stumbles through the snow to the river and out onto the ice, where she faints and drifts toward the falls. David pursues her through the woods onto the ice from floe to floe and scoops her to safety at the last moment.

The final sequences were shot under great difficulty and hardship for the actors and crew alike. Griffith waited for a real snowstorm, and he later found a real ice floe. Miss Gish prepared herself daily to work in the cold weather and took cold baths for weeks. After months of waiting, through December, January, and February, the needed blizzard came in March and the company rushed into it. It was a sizable storm. To hold the camera upright, three men lay on the ground gripping the legs of its tripod. Filming required day and night work, and at one point Miss Gish actually fainted. She was revived and the filming continued. The camera froze. Faces froze. For the river scenes, the company went to White River Junction, Vermont, and, before all the needed shots were taken, Miss Gish had become a slab of ice at least twenty times a day for two weeks, her face and hands exposed and her hair usually trailing in the water.

The final rescue from the ice was shot later in the year at Farm-

Lillian Gish on the (real) ice floe in Way Down East.

ington, Connecticut, with painted wooden blocks substituting for ice. At one point, Barthelmess moved a bit too slowly; he jumped onto a block that was too small and it dropped him into the icy water; he nearly missed Miss Gish at the top of the falls. When Miss Gish prepared for her final scene, where she is carried to a cabin by David after the rescue, she presented herself as she was from the river—her hair stringy, wet, her face half-frozen. No, Griffith told her. The climax is over. The audience will want to see you beautiful again. Make up. Comb your hair. When she protested that it would not be real, he spoke to her angrily, "Don't tell me how to make motion pictures! Hurry up and do as you're told! This picture has to make money! Now go and make yourself pretty." The film was indeed a success with the public, and, particularly considering the simplicity and crudeness of the original conception of Anna, Lillian Gish's performance is exceptional. The virtues of *Way Down East* are the virtues of a highly skillful, first-rate, intuitive filmmaker at work, but the force of genius is not in it.

In Griffith's next film less skill is evident, and less first-rate filmmaking. It was called *Dream Street* and was conceived as a kind of follow-up to *Broken Blossoms,* based on two more of the tales from Burke's *Limehouse Nights* collection. In execution, *Dream Street* was a badly conceived amalgam of realism, melodrama, allegory, and poetic atmosphere. The cast, headed by Carol Dempster, was not up to the very difficult assignment. Symbolic sequences—visions of Heaven, Hell, the Crucifixion—seem to most observers like pretentious parodies of Griffith's best use of similar effects. And most audiences find the leading characters in *Dream Street* rather uninteresting and didactic representatives of good or evil, rather than real people.

Griffith opened the film at the Central Theatre in New York on April 12, 1921 and ran it there for four weeks. He then moved it to Town Hall, newly renovated for film exhibition, and he experimented with synchronized sound (music and effects recorded on discs) added to the film. He appeared on screen himself also, speaking a kind of prologue.

Griffith and journalist H. M. Van Tine on the White House steps in 1921 to invite President Woodrow Wilson to see Way Down East.

Sound was not new to films. In his superb book, *The Silent Clowns,* Walter Kerr explains that the possibility of sound films, and even talking films, as we now know them, had existed almost from the beginning. The possibilities lay undeveloped because esthetically hardly anyone was interested. Edison had experimented with a combination of his phonograph and his kinetoscope quite early, and some models had appeared in penny arcades with moving pictures seen through viewer and synchronized sound heard through forceps-like earphones. There were subsequent efforts at sound films too, and subsequent systems and techniques tried out for use of sound with theatrical films. Several years after *Dream Street,* Warner Brothers again revived the idea of a synchronous sound-on-disc, first with short films and then (for music and sound effects only) in 1926 for a John Barrymore film called *Don Juan.* The following year, the same studio issued *The Jazz Singer* with Al Jolson, which had some songs and some dialogue scenes as well. Only then did the public flock to see and *hear* a movie.

Ten

Orphans of the Storm
and
Isn't Life Wonderful

The filming on *Dream Street* done, D. W. Griffith announced that he would undertake a version of *Faust* to star Lillian Gish as Marguerite. Miss Gish herself had misgivings. *Faust,* she discovered, had never found favor with American audiences. She confided her feelings to Harry Carr, a long-time Griffith associate, whose job it was to find ideas and stories for possible production. Carr shared her feelings: *Faust* would be another chance for Griffith to preach, to be sure, but what he needed was a money-maker. Miss Gish approached Mr. Griffith. So did Carr. Griffith was dissuaded. She had a counter-proposition, a play even older than *Way Down East* called *The Two Orphans* about two "adopted" sisters, one blind, who became separated in a teeming city. It had been filmed before, actually, in a short version of 1911 by Selig, and in 1915 as a vehicle for Theda Bara. Miss Bara had risen to immediate public favor playing *femme fatale,* "vamp" roles first in *A Fool There Was,* and she had wanted to try something else.

Griffith's mind went to work on *The Two Orphans.* He wanted to expand on the story so that he could produce another spectacle. He decided to transpose the action to Paris at the time of the French Revolution. The social turmoil made the difficulties of the separation of the sisters more believable and more urgent. It also gave Griffith a legitimate reason to include mob scenes, duels, executions, fighting, and a last-minute rescue from the guillotine. It is quite possible also that he was influenced by the success in America of *Madame Du Barry,* a film by the great German director Ernst Lubitsch.

Griffith researched his project thoroughly, down to the small detail of how Robespierre had actually walked. And Dickens's novel of the French Revolution, *A Tale of Two Cities,* was never far from his mind. When production began, the director had fourteen acres of sets thrown up on the Marmaroneck peninsula, reproducing Paris streets, along with replicas of Notre Dame, Versailles, and the Bastille. He hired a costume designer. He cast Lillian Gish as Henriette and Dorothy Gish as her blind adopted sister, Louise. He gave Joseph Schildkraut his first film role as the male lead. Although in his way Griffith this time tried to be careful about costs, he spent a great deal of money—more than he had on *Way Down East.* He opened his completed film in late December of 1921 in Boston and a few days later in New York.

Orphans of the Storm, as the film was finally called, is the work of a first-rate filmmaker. There are, as Iris Barry has pointed out, minor irritations—some of the subtitles, and the occasionally awkward (but theatrically conventional) way Dorothy Gish uses a vague stare to indicate her blindness. There are some comic touches that don't work, there is (inevitably) the highly sentimental nature of the main plot, and, to some, the final rescue may seem a bit protracted. In its original "road show" at advance prices, *Orphans of the Storm* was shown in two parts. The first is full of Griffith-devised incidents, beside the separation of the sisters, which was already there. There are duels, orgies (mild orgies, to be sure, even compared to *Intolerance*), a murder, a kidnapping. There is also a scene in which Henriette overhears the voice of the blind and lost Louise singing in the streets. Audiences found the latter so vivid that they were convinced they heard Dorothy Gish's song. In the second half, Griffith portrayed the Revolution, and he did it magnificently.

Street scene from Orphans of the Storm.

Eileen Bowser comments that "the streaming mobs are as frighten-
ing as the Clan ride in *The Birth of a Nation,* and the storming of
the Bastille, the masses surging into the streets and squares, with
torches and weapons held aloft, must be counted with Griffith's best
work." In some shots Griffith masked off the top and bottom of his
screen, as he had in *The Birth of a Nation,* to show us the thrust
of a horse charge or of a crowd. In this he was, of course, anticipat-
ing the ratio of wide-screen, but, more important, he was making
the size and shape of his screen a flexible aspect of his drama.

Orphans of the Storm is a vivid and effective film, but there is
truth in Lewis Jacobs' assertion that it is the work of a man "no
longer influencing the movies but being influenced by them." It
was photographed by Hendrick Sartov and Paul Allen; Bitzer did
not participate, and indeed would participate intermittently and only

A song the audience was sure it could hear. Dorothy (below) and Lillian Gish in Orphans of the Storm.

collaboratively on Griffith films from this point on. He had begun
drinking heavily. He was, some say, jealous of Sartov's presence and
growing importance; but Bitzer had always been jealous of the
work of other cameramen assigned to him as assistants and associates, beginning with Karl Brown. Bitzer was also increasingly de-
pressed by his own domestic situation. Griffith understood his plight,
and Bitzer, for his part, knew he had become impossible to work
with and never held his own decline against the director. It is somewhat ironic that *Orphans of the Storm* was also Lillian Gish's last
film with Griffith, for it was she who had first brought in Sartov.
She went on, with Griffith's blessing, to a career of her own.

Orphans of the Storm was not as big a success with the public as
Griffith hoped it would be, or needed it to be. There was an additional expense beyond production costs because William Fox, who
had produced the Theda Bara version, had the foreign rights to the
story and held up Griffith's London opening until an $85,000 settle-
ment was awarded him. Similarly, when Griffith announced his
film, an imported Italian version of *The Two Orphans* was being
widely shown in the United States, and this probably took away
some of his potential audience. Furthermore, there were losses from
the first "road show" release in large theaters at advance prices. The
practice had paid off for Griffith as recently as *Broken Blossoms* and
Way Down East, but it brought losses to *Orphans of the Storm* and
subsequent Griffith films. Nevertheless, Griffith continued to use
"road show" presentations. He had put in charge his brother Albert
(who had taken the professional name of Albert Grey) and Albert
did not manage these road shows or their publicity very well. So, the
losses were partly a matter of family loyalty, and family loyalty and
close Southern family ties were an important part of Griffith's life.
Indeed, he supported improvident brothers, sisters, and nephews all
of his life. Despite his 16- to 24-hour days, and the virtually 365-day
years that Griffith had devoted to film since 1908, he had always
taken the time to visit his family in Kentucky regularly. Indeed, his
mother's death in the year of *The Birth of a Nation* undoubtedly
had an effect on the sincerity of that film.

After *Orphans of the Storm,* Griffith considered producing a grandiose film in England with a script by H. G. Wells, to be based on his *Outline of History,* with the purpose of promoting the League of Nations. But the project came to nothing, even though Griffith made a quick trip to London in its interests. The next project turned out to be a programmer with Carol Dempster and Henry Hull called *One Exciting Night,* a mystery concocted by Griffith. It was partly based on old movie serials, dime novels, and the popularity of Broadway successes in the genre that came to be called "old dark house thrillers" like *The Bat* and *The Cat and the Canary* which featured secret passageways, clutching hands from sliding panels, and the rest. *One Exciting Night* is credited with being the screen's first such atmospheric mystery-thriller. One of its major sequences came about by accident. A hurricane struck Mamaroneck on June 11, 1922, and Griffith rushed his cameramen out of doors and wrote the storm into the climax of his story. An offensive aspect of the film today is the presence of "Romeo Washington," the "frightened Negro," played in blackface by Porter Strong. The character had been common enough until fairly recently in film, stage play, comic strip, and novel (and appears in Griffith's *The Greatest Question* and *Dream Street,* too) and few whites seem to have been aware a racial insult might be involved.

Next Griffith announced that he was giving up spectacle films. The disappointing returns from *Orphans of the Storm* were much on his mind. He undertook a Southern rural tale, shot on location in Louisiana and Florida, called *The White Rose.* It featured Carol Dempster, and also Mae Marsh in a reunion with Griffith that both of them had looked forward to. Her career had gradually declined since she left the director, but her performance here is outstanding. Alas, it could not save the film. And not much can be said for the other performances. Griffith himself said later of *The White Rose,* "I do not think that the picture we made did amount to very much. Some of the best things in it emanated from the atmosphere where the moss hung along the Bayou Teche." The picture has an old fashioned plot, full of the strong sentiment and the unlikely plot coincidences of Griffith's best rural tales. At the same time, the director made an effort of sorts to keep up with the times by including some mid-1920s "flappers" and introducing an awkward, over-played hip waggle by several of his female bit players. Nor was the film helped by the fact that it had to do with a Christian minister fallen from grace; ministerial organizations generally objected to it and in some areas it was banned.

During a showing of *The White Rose,* the rising director Henry King visited Griffith backstage to pay his respects. Griffith told him, "My boy, you're too good. You were too good in *Tol'able David.* You're giving me a rough race." King considered it the highest compliment he was ever to receive. *Tol'able David* is of course a

Griffith directs Mae Marsh and Ivor Novello in The White Rose.

classic film of rural America. Griffith himself had suggested the story to its star Richard Barthelmess when they parted company. King also directed Ronald Colman and Lillian Gish in her first film after she and Griffith parted, *The White Sister,* at the beginning of a long and distinguished directorial career. Another remarkable event in Griffith's career at this point involved Al Jolson, who was having continued success on the musical stage. Griffith approached him and arranged for a test on a $100,000 stage especially constructed for the singer. Jolson saw the test, and never returned to the Mamaroneck studio or explained his absence, although production on a Jolson feature was set for the following Monday and a crew was standing by.

Griffith next returned to historical spectacle. With a fanfare of publicity that contrasted sharply with the secrecy that had attended the planning of *The Birth of a Nation,* he announced that he would film the story of the American Revolution and call it *America.* The aid of historians and historical societies was solicited; the Daughters of the American Revolution cooperated; the army lent troops. And Griffith returned to some of the library research he had done as a young would-be playwright in New York. A sub-plot was written for Carol Dempster and a young Neil Hamilton, then at the beginning of his career. Lionel Barrymore was cast as the cruel British Captain Walter Butler. Griffith made him the villain of the piece, but as an individual, not as a representative of England's policies.

"Test your patriotism—see *America!*" wrote one reviewer. "Audience appeal 100%," said a theater manager. But it was not so. *America* was not a success, and it took many years of reissue and the sale of "stock footage" of its battle scenes (which were used to fill out cheaper productions) for it even to earn back its cost. Those battle scenes were brilliantly staged, but somehow insensitively edited. The sub-plot, the "love interest," was uninteresting. The subtitles, full of long historical explanations and rationalizations, seemed to take up half the film. James Quirk, editor of the then respected *Photoplay* magazine (in those years a kind of model of what an intelligent, well-edited "fan" magazine might be), wrote an editorial which addressed Griffith:

> You have made yourself an anchorite at Mamaroneck. . . . Your pictures shape themselves toward a certain brutality because of this austerity. . . . Your refusal to face the world is making you more and more a sentimentalist. You see passion in terms of cooing doves or the falling of a rose petal. . . . Your lack of contact with life makes you deficient in humor. In other words, your splendid unsophistication is a menace to you—and to pictures.

Whether Quirk perceived the causes correctly or not, he expressed the feelings of many about Griffith in 1924. Lillian Gish saw *America* at Mamaroneck and found it for the most part a heartbreaking disappointment. Griffith, she felt, no longer had anyone to say "no" to him. She knew that he thrived on the gentle abrasion of those who tactfully questioned his ideas or hinted at alternate ways. Griffith seems to have felt this, for he now constantly questioned his associates and asked for advice. "Well, what would you do?" and "What do you think of it?" were questions that echoed back through his career to the earliest days at Biograph and, although many felt he asked such questions only perfunctorily and without intending to heed the answers, the truth was that he needed a gentle and concerned antagonist in order to clarify his own thinking. Now, he had around him only "yes men."

Financial problems had become enormous, and in order to make his next film, Griffith undertook a move that would eventually cost him his independence. He had been quarreling constantly with the management at United Artists because he was convinced that the company's releasing contracts were unfavorable to him. The U.A. executives, however, were able to demonstrate that his films lost money. Nevertheless, the company made public announcements that the original contracts of the partnership were being renewed and all was well. For his part, Griffith saw such announcements merely as a show put on for the public, and, particularly, for others in the film business. He approached Adolph Zukor at Paramount and signed a releasing contract with him, thereby gaining partial backing from Zukor for a film to be shot in Germany called *Isn't Life Wonderful*. So he set sail with his cast, which included Carol Dempster and Neil Hamilton. When Zukor issued an announcement that Griffith was now under contract to produce for Paramount, United Artists was, of course, furious.

Isn't Life Wonderful was suggested to Griffith by his financial manager, J. C. "Little" Epping, who had retained his German citizenship and had relatives in Germany. It was a story of the straits that Germany's citizens found themselves in after World War I. Griffith also saw it as a way of making up for the way he had treated the Germans in *Hearts of the World*. Even the villains of the story were working men made criminal by hunger. *Isn't Life Wonderful* is an unusually restrained film for Griffith—in its performances (some by non-professionals), in its lack of contrivance, in its photography, and in its editing. Hunger, malnutrition, and bread riots are portrayed with striking realism. It was influential, too, in theme and treatment on subsequent filmmaking in Germany and the rest of Europe. According to Eileen Bowser, it was "Griffith's last great film."

The director now became a Paramount employee. To gain his services, the company had paid off his most pressing debts. It also put him on a salary of $6,000 a week, but, as Griffith said later, much of this went to pay off other debts. For example, he owed Hendrick Sartov $10,000 in back salary, and eventually paid it all. "I am working for nothing," Griffith said at one point. Paramount announced the acquisition of its new director in full-page ads that showed romantically-rendered portraits of Griffith surrounded by scenes from his more famous films. The pompous copy read, "There is a point in the life of every great artist when, if he is free from cares, he can produce his greatest works. Everything before, however distinguished, serves as preparation. Some critics feel they can pick out the place where Shakespeare's art reached its greatest pe-

The bread line scene from Isn't Life Wonderful.

riod. So it is with the master director David Wark Griffith, who is at work on a series of Paramount Pictures. In freedom from all worry and with the resources of the world's foremost film organization at his disposal, D. W. Griffith is now in the golden age of his art." Griffith was eased into his position as a Paramount employee. He did not have to move again to California but only nearby to part of Long Island, the company's studios at Astoria. And at this early point, the California Paramount brass sometimes still deferred to his ideas. He was still a leader in the film world despite the state of his career.

Griffith suggested a film with the vaudeville and Broadway comedian, W. C. Fields, a version of his great stage success, *Poppy,* a show which had established for Fields the rapscallion, con-man character that he was to play variations upon so brilliantly for the rest of his career. Fields had made a few film appearances before —in a couple of one-reel comedies made in the States by a French company, and later as a comic British officer in *Janice Meredith,* a Marion Davies vehicle about the American Revolution—but neither had established him in films. Much of what Fields did in his first Griffith film, re-titled *Sally of the Sawdust,* surely came from his stage performances—his bits of business with a cigar, his inventive sleight of hand, and the rest. But there is a hilarious, bumping, run-away ride in a Ford car that is pure film comedy. We are apt to think of Fields as a great comedian of sound film, but he made eight silent features after *Sally of the Sawdust,* and with the rediscovery of some of these early Fields films, "lost" for many years, Fields is now being acclaimed as an outstanding silent comedian.

As it turned out, neither *Isn't Life Wonderful* nor *Sally of the Sawdust* was released by Paramount. Griffith had to arrange to turn them over to United Artists for distribution to fulfill his obligation to that company. They were also Griffith's farewell to a degree of independence. For he now became just another director in the employ of a big studio, obliged to make the films assigned to him with the actors offered him, keep to the budget, and bring them in on time.

Griffith next brought in two films produced under great pressure and with the further pressure of a developing conflict of orders and instructions from Paramount executives. Indeed, some critics have wondered whether the producers, now fully holding the power in the film business, had not deliberately set out to destroy Griffith's career. *That Royle Girl* was based on a story that featured murder, gangsters, a storm, and a disreputable road house, all in a script which had been at Paramount for years and had been turned down by one director after another. Griffith was persuaded to undertake it and to include a part for W. C. Fields as well. (Paramount knew what it had in the Fields of *Sally of the Sawdust.*) The film began as a programmer. When officials decided it needed something extra,

W. C. Fields and Carol Dempster in Sally of the Sawdust.

a $100,000 cyclone was added, which ran Griffith's picture well over its budget. During production, Lillian Gish visited Griffith in Astoria and, as usual, asked to see rushes of the film he was working on. He acted embarrassed and begged off. He had fifty bosses now, he protested, but at least he was paying his debts. Next Griffith undertook *The Sorrows of Satan,* a property that had originally been bought for director Cecil B. De Mille, an outstanding Paramount showman for years, who had left, over disagreements with the higher-ups, to form his own company. It was announced as a "big" picture, but the conflicting orders from various executives—directives given and countermanded, from Hollywood to Astoria—made a shambles of its budget. Griffith's finished film was re-edited and its sequences re-shuffled under orders from one group of Paramount front-office officials. Then Zukor himself intervened and somehow blamed Griffith for allowing such conflicts to affect his work. A box office disaster resulted, and Griffith again was blamed. Seeing *The Sorrows of Satan* today, one realizes that Griffith's heart was indeed in many of its scenes—a symbolic prologue representing the battle of the angels and the Fall of Satan (abbreviated in the released version, however) and scenes of poverty showing the heroine and hero in a shabby rooming house, which might well have come from the memory of his own early days in New York.

Griffith directs Carol Dempster in The Sorrows of Satan.

The film ended Griffith's association with Paramount. He then seriously considered joining Cecil B. De Mille's effort at independence, the Producer's Distributing Company. Griffith's core of associates was alarmed, and advised him against the move. They proved to have been right, for De Mille's effort soon failed, and he had to return to Zukor and Paramount. There also was a rumor that Griffith would sign with Universal—a minor studio in those days: a

Griffith, theater owner Sig Grauman, Carl Laemmle, Jr., and Universal's version of sound-on-film, "the Unitone."

move there would have confirmed Griffith's fall from prominence. The rumor spoke of offers to direct versions of *Uncle Tom's Cabin* and *Show Boat*. But it was only a rumor.

In early 1927, Griffith returned to United Artists, but not to independence. The company had not done well, both as a result of the fate of Griffith's pictures and also because the other partners— Fairbanks, Pickford, and Chaplin—had not made enough films to keep it supplied. Put in charge was producer Joseph Schenck, who was married to Norma Talmadge, was brother-in-law to the brilliant comedian Buster Keaton, and had his own group of stars. He put United Artists on its feet, unquestionably, and re-hired Griffith, but not to work independently for United Artists, as before. Griffith was to produce for Schenck's own Art Cinema Corporation which distributed through United Artists, and he was to be very much under Schenck's direct supervision. The move also meant that Griffith had to return to Hollywood—a Hollywood that had changed a great deal since he left it nine years before.

Eleven

Return to Hollywood

It will not quite do to say (as has often been said) that after 1916 the men who gradually assumed power in the movies knew nothing about making films but a great deal about making money. Those usually mentioned include Adolph Zukor (ex-furrier), Louis B. Mayer (ex-junk-dealer), Jesse L. Lasky (ex-cornetist), Sam Goldfish (later Goldwyn, an ex-glove-salesman), William Fox (ex-cloth-shrinker)—the new controlling producers. But it had become evident that there were millions of people waiting for the movies to come to them, huge theaters to be built, and thousands of pictures to be made, and the men to do all this, with varying amounts and kinds of taste and talent, were basically businessmen-gamblers, eager to accept the challenges of filling houses and reaching audiences. Griffith eventually suffered because of the system they installed. We simply do not know (and cannot know) what would have become of John Ford or Eric von Stroheim or Raoul Walsh or Henry King or William Wellman or Richard Barthelmess—or their audiences— without these producers. "I'm not a bad business man, honestly I'm not," Griffith protested on his return to Hollywood. "I was never in difficulties until I turned my business over to others. In California, in the old days, when I both directed and managed, I got along all right. It was only when I came to Mamaroneck and turned over my business handlings to others. . . . Of course, the collapse of everything at Mamaroneck nearly broke my heart. We missed success so narrowly. Bad management and bad releasing contracts caused the destruction." But was it really a matter of who ran his business affairs, whether bankers in New York or producers in Hollywood?

In any case, the greater question now was whether a creative and intuitive artist such as Griffith could continue to function as a part of a mass art and a mass business; whether he could function within a studio set-up now complex and standardized. With the help of his actors and carpenters and cameramen, Griffith had made film a personal expression. No matter how many people had been involved in a Griffith film "in the old days," Griffith's intuitive genius was the inspiration and the arbiter of everything. Now, writers, production designers, art directors, costume designers, make-up men, and others were all taking a direct hand. The director remained the maker of movies, but he no longer mattered so much until the filming started, and even then he might have a producer standing behind him. Griffith had sampled this new system when he worked for Paramount at Astoria. But now the supervision was direct, with meetings and conferences and even confrontations on the set in place of telegrams and letters.

There was sizable irony in the fact that Griffith, as we have seen, was the man who had given this mass art its style and its prestige. He had made it possible, but clearly his future within it was now in doubt. Further, there was the question of whether an artist of late Victorian sensibilities could continue to appeal to the public in the "Jazz Age." At least superficially—and perhaps profoundly— the United States had changed a great deal in the ten short years between 1918 and 1928. So D. W. Griffith was in danger of going out of style, whether or not he was running out of art. More than one commentator has observed of Griffith's best films that they evoke emotions through pictures that a great writer could not hope to evoke with words. But at this time Griffith himself was feeling that "writers are the only ones who can express their ego. Directors can't because they have to please the majority. We can't deal with opinions. All we can do is to weave a little romance as pleasantly as we know how."

There were people in Hollywood who had not wished Griffith well when he had left. Some had been jealous of his prestigious position, however much they respected—or said they respected—his talent and the importance of his work. Some felt that in leaving he was behaving as though he thought himself too good for Hollywood and for the rest of the film world. He had, after all, frequently succeeded when many in the industry predicted he would fail, and he had brought in ridiculously expensive films that became great successes. It is never easy to be proven wrong. At any rate, Griffith was now back, and Schenck first put the great man to work salvaging Del Lord's film, called *Topsy and Eva*—a variation and mild spoof of *Uncle Tom's Cabin,* starring Rosetta and Eva, the Duncan Sisters—shooting some additional scenes and re-editing the result, all anonymously. That accomplished, Griffith and Schenck set about to produce three films, all obviously aimed straight at the box office, and all with sex themes.

Drums of Love, the first of them, is a story of adultery, laid in the Italy of the nineteenth century. A slow, slick, competently and almost anonymously directed studio film, it opens with some good battle scenes, which probably could have been made by any able director imitating Griffith's earlier work. Then it settles in on monotonous close-ups of the principals, Mary Philbin and Don Alvarado, who had beautiful faces but a range of about two expressions. Its heroine, quite un-Griffith-like, clearly provokes her own seduction. Eileen Bowser comments, "the camera movements that describe her consciousness of her own sexual appeal are very skillful and show Griffith as less prudish than usual." The film was badly titled by Gervit Lloyd, who had been a publicity man working with Griffith, but contains a good bravura performance by Lionel Barrymore. The plot once ended with the deaths of the principals, hardly good box office for such a story. A second, "happy" ending was shot and it was incongruous. Griffith, now willing to fit his films to circumstance, instructed his staff to eliminate certain scenes from the prints shown to state censorship boards and then re-insert them in the versions sent out to theaters, but United Artists refused to go along.

When the film premiered in New York on January 24, 1928, the director appeared before the curtain and said in broken tones to the audience that he supposed he had produced another film that wouldn't mean much to the box office. "I haven't any brains, I guess, as far as that part of the business is concerned. And although I really intended to try and hit public approval with this piece, I went ahead and did something different again. I am glad if you like it." It was one of the few occasions when Griffith allowed a lack of inner confidence to be seen in public.

D. W. Griffith had never been ill, his associates attest, except with an occasional cold. But colds were a preoccupation with him. He practiced his boxing every morning he could and took frequent cold baths, sometimes with ice added to the water. No one with the hint of a cold was allowed close to Griffith. But now he often pleaded "a slight cold" to keep himself away from others. It was often not a cold, but the fear they would smell the alcohol on him. Since his return to California D. W. Griffith had begun drinking too much. And there was little point in his trying to cover it up, for most people in the film business knew it.

His next film was an up-dated remake of the little pot-boiler he had hurriedly ground out for Reliance-Majestic in 1914, *The Battle of the Sexes*. In the original, the gowns of the "siren" had modestly touched the tops of her shoes. Thirteen years later, Phyllis Haver, in the same part, wore dresses that hit her above the knee, and the camera angles often showed off that fact. It should be made clear, however, that, if Griffith was willing to make films on the subject of sex in an effort to renew his career, he was not quite willing to exploit the subject. He had been shocked when the actress Mar-

guerite Clark in *Wildflower,* at the beginning of her career, had
taken off her stocking before the camera. And he had been appalled
when Cecil B. De Mille, in filming *Joan the Woman* on the life of
Joan of Arc, had added a love affair to her early life.

By now, Hollywood—catching up to the Griffith of *Dream
Street*—was in the midst of a changeover to sound film, and a recorded musical score and sound effects were added to the remake of
The Battle of the Sexes. There were two methods of recording
sound for films at the time. There was the Warner Brothers "Vita-
phone" sound-on-disc method with large 16-inch phonograph records—essentially the system Griffith had tried out with *Dream Street*
in 1921. The more satisfactory method, and the one eventually
adopted by all, involved adding a light-sensitive sound-track to the
film itself, which, among other advantages, made synchronization
automatic. The method was basically similar to Lee DeForest's
"Phonofilm" which had been used for "novelty" theatrical short subjects since the early twenties. Popular early sound-on-disc films, including Jolson's pivotal *The Jazz Singer,* were later re-recorded with
sound-on-film, and are thus preserved, but many less popular disc-
recorded films were not re-done, and the discs have been lost. And
so it was with *The Battle of the Sexes.* So it was also with Griffith's
next film, *Lady of the Pavements,* for which a few sequences of
dialogue and song were shot for the leading lady, Lupe Velez, making it (like several films of the time), a "part-talkie." The film and
its script had been prepared for director Sam Taylor, but then
Schenck assigned it to Griffith. It was a Ruritanian tale of an affair
between Count and commoner. Griffith wanted to record his sound
for this film realistically by having the volume of Miss Velez's voice
increase or decrease as she moved toward or away from the camera,
but this proved to be beyond the resources of his technicians. The
camera credit on *Lady of the Pavements* read "photographed by
Karl Struss assisted by G. W. Bitzer." Struss did a great deal to give
Griffith's films of this period a slick, fashionable studio sheen. As for
Bitzer, he was losing his bout with the bottle, and this was the last

Griffith film on which he worked. He drifted onto the fringes of the film business, taking whatever work he could get, and ended up on a W.P.A. film project in the early years of the Depression. After New York's Museum of Modern Art Film Library was founded in 1935, Bitzer served as an early advisor. He died in 1944.

Griffith, by 1930, was so thoroughly discouraged by United Artists that he threatened to leave. His friends, feeling that departure would have meant financial disaster for him, dissuaded him. Griffith had been reluctant about the dialogue film, the "talkie," and with good reason. He felt that film pantomime was a universal language that dialogue could only make limited and insular. By 1930, however, it was clear that the talkies were here, and to stay, and Griffith was beginning to talk of them as a challenge. Furthermore, there was a feeling in the industry that it was perhaps time for a "comeback" by the great director in the new medium. Griffith had been reading *John Brown's Body,* Steven Vincent Benét's effort to write an epic poem about the American Civil War. He wanted to make a film of it.

"What are you talking about?" The U. A. bigwigs wanted to know. "You can't make a movie out of a poem."

"I've done it before. I did it with *Pippa Passes."*

"Well, that was a long time ago. People would watch anything then."

"But Benét is a recognized writer. This book won a Pulitzer Prize."

"What's that to the average moviegoer?"

Finally settled upon was an ambitious biographical film on Abraham Lincoln, a subject satisfactory to all, and very close to Griffith's heart. "I'll probably have to wheel in a Pulmotor [a respirator] after he's been assassinated," the director cracked privately, "so we can have a happy ending." Reportedly, Carl Sandburg was approached to write a script but he wanted more than Schenck was willing to pay. In the end, Benét himself was hired. So were Walter Huston to play Lincoln, Una Merkel to be Ann Rutledge, and Kay

Hammond for Mary Todd. Benét's agreement specified that he would write his script in complete independence of the studio bosses—he had been warned about the ways of Hollywood. But after he had finished, the bosses insisted on a script conference. Benét sat through a dissection of his work in silence. When the producers' remarks were over he looked at Griffith, shook his head sadly, picked up his hat, left the studio, took the next train back to his home in the East, and was not heard from again.

Abraham Lincoln emerged on the screen as an episodic treatment of events in the life of the President. A similarly loose structure later produced excellent biographical movies—Charles Laughton's films on Henry VIII and Rembrandt, for example. Those films succeed partly because individual scenes have great vitality and are parts of a carefully evolving revelation of character through conflict. In Griffith's *Lincoln,* we often feel we are watching formal and stilted vignettes, illustrating historical events. Certain basic production details so attentively watched over in Griffith's best films, are neglected in this one. The sets do not look lived in; the clothes do not look previously worn; the locales do not seem familiar to the characters. Many of the scenes look hastily put together, probably because pressures from Griffith's bosses—plus his own dissatisfaction—dictated constant changes in his script. But *Abraham Lincoln* is not without its virtues. Some of the early rural scenes are beautifully rendered, despite Una Merkel's strange characterization of Ann Rutledge. And Huston has some fine moments: the scene where he receives the news of Ann's death has often been admired. So have the scenes of Northern and Southern soldiers marching off to fight, and of General Sheridan's ride to rally his troops.

Some of *Lincoln*'s virtues have to do with a truly creative use of sound. When Hollywood turned to sound, it briefly turned its back on its own esthetic—or at least some of its directors did. They returned to the stage for a model, as filmmakers had in the earliest days, and produced some slow, talky, and stilted films. The more perceptive directors, however, realized that they were still dealing

D. W. Griffith and Stephen Vincent Benét.

with a visual medium and that the techniques pioneered by Griffith were effective. (These directors, incidentally, were not always experienced film men—Rouben Mamoulian, for example, imported along with many others from the stage, produced a brilliantly cinematic film in his first movie, *Applause* with Helen Morgan.) Griffith in his *Lincoln* remained true to some of his own first principles of good cinema. And he used sound to underline effective visuals, sometimes shooting with a moving camera and recording his sound later, if necessary. There is also a moving and creative use of the sound track. In a sequence involving Lincoln's political campaigning, off-screen sounds counterpoint the visuals. We begin with a series of "lap" (overlapping) dissolves of on-camera campaign oratory. These involve bits of the Lincoln-Douglas debates, and show us Houston and E. Alyn Warren on campaign platforms. We cut to a pan across the objects in a lonely, almost empty hotel room. The camera pauses briefly on a stovepipe hat, as Lincoln, off camera, is heard faintly, still delivering a speech. The camera in motion picks up Mary Todd Lincoln seated patiently. The camera waits until an obviously exhausted Lincoln enters. Outside, the hubbub of campaigning continues, subdued on the sound-track; bands blare, stridently forced cheers go up.

"I'm home, Mary," the campaigner says wearily.

"You must be tired, dear," she answers with simple domesticity. "Sit down. I'll get your supper."

What many directors of early "talkies," Griffith included, did not grasp was pace. When visuals are complemented and underlined by dialogue and sound, pace needs to be quickened.

Griffith said that directing *Lincoln* was "a nightmare of the mind and nerves." When his own shooting was finished (but before some miniatures, other special effects, and the editing were done), he left for Mineral Wells, Texas, which had become a favorite retreat. Thus he saw the film for the first time at its New York opening, October 25, 1930. As usual, he wanted to do some further editing, but his ideas were rejected. *Abraham Lincoln* was at first well reviewed, made some money for United Artists, and briefly restored Griffith's prestige. By the time it was released, Griffith and Schenck had agreed to settle their differences by parting company and let a fifth contracted picture be forgotten. *Lincoln* was, Griffith said at the time, the proverbial situation of too many cooks spoiling the broth. He was less proverbial and more specific in a letter to Schenck which he wrote but never sent. It had been a mistake, he said, to reject Benét's script with its subsidiary love story. The film would have had meaning for audiences and still the presentation of Lincoln would not have been hurt. Indeed, it would have given a plotless film a plot. When Lincoln pardons the soldier in the "tent scene," Griffith continued, he would have pardoned someone whom

Abraham Lincoln (Walter Huston) and his Secretary of War (Oscar Apfel).

we all knew and loved. It would also have given us some suspense as to what was going to happen to at least two of our characters until the very end. "Lincoln, after all, could furnish little suspense. The audience already knows what is going to happen to him." It was a little late to be saying all this, to be sure. But Griffith's intuitive temperament could rarely indulge in such reasoned critical comment *before* the fact. The creative intuition does not do well to edit and criticize itself while it is active. Perhaps the man who could deal with small businessmen and produce *The Musketeers of Pig Alley,* simply could not both deal with big businessmen and produce anything at all. Or perhaps all the years of trying to deal with businessmen had simply broken Griffith as an artist, beyond repair.

Griffith had rested, then, during all the post-production work on *Abraham Lincoln*. He believed his failures had occurred because he had not been given a free hand. He was working for others who left him little say in his own work. If he could manage to produce a film on his own, preferably in the East, away from Hollywood, he could succeed again. The change did come. It seems that the D. W. Griffith Company had made a tax overpayment in 1920, and in 1929 the Treasury Department issued a refund. This money was quietly invested by the company treasurer, and, despite the Depression, the investment had done well. This money, plus a small bank loan, and an advance from United Artists in return for distribution rights, would enable the director to make a modest film if he worked quickly. Griffith chose a story by Emile Zola called *The Drunkard*. He wanted a script that would expose some of the evils of Prohibition and the poisonous nature of bootleg whiskey, as well as make a comment on alcoholism. His associates felt that Prohibition was a dead issue—unworkable and obviously destined to be shortly re-

Griffith prepares to photograph and record a scene for The Struggle.

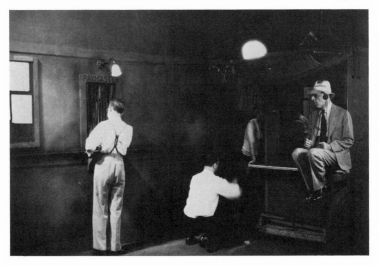

pealed. Anita Loos, along with her husband John Emerson, rejoined Griffith to work on the script, but she was convinced that the only way to treat the subject was as a comedy. She thought of Jimmy Durante and told Griffith so. He even considered the idea but rejected it.

Griffith's film came to be titled *The Struggle*. The director shot hastily. He had hoped to be able to use the Paramount Long Island studios, but the deal fell through, and he was forced to rent the old Biograph Studios in the Bronx, where he had completed *Judith of Bethulia* in 1913. Equipment was poor. Some of the location scenes shot in the Bronx streets and at the Stamford Rolling Mills in Springdale, Connecticut, are vivid. Some of the close-ups of Hal Skelly's tortured face as the hero are superb. Griffith's effort to make his dialogue colloquial and realistic, in a time when film writing was often overly "clever" and when dialogue was often delivered with stilted, "theatrical" diction, is commendable. But otherwise, the acting in *The Struggle* is inadequate. The meaning is muddled—is the film a comment on alcoholism or on the absurdity of Prohibition and the fact that it produced poisonous whiskey? Would Skelly's alcoholism have been acceptable on good whiskey legally obtained? The plot is thin (and rather like Griffith's early Biograph *The Drunkard's Reformation*); the use of speech only makes Griffith's melodrama seem exaggerated and absurd. The sets seem shabby but unreal. At best, Griffith was attempting to copy himself.

The Struggle opened in New York on December 10, 1931. Audiences laughed at the wrong places. Its press notices were terrible. One trade paper refused to review it out of respect for Griffith. The director was shattered. He hid in his hotel room. United Artists quietly withdrew *The Struggle* from circulation after a week. Shortly afterward, the D. W. Griffith Company went into bankruptcy. Twenty-one of his films were auctioned. The highest bidder was Griffith himself. He acquired them all for $500.

Twelve

A Long Neglect

In 1932, D. W. Griffith became 58 years old (although, if one were to believe some of his earlier press releases, he was only 53). He was to live for sixteen years more, but he was never again to make a film of his own. And the man who worked so hard and long and eagerly for so many years would find, toward the end, that there was no work at all. There were plans—always there were plans. At first they were sizable. He was going to be appointed head of production for R.K.O. Pictures. He was working on a play about the American Revolution (but that plan, as we know, went back three decades). *Intolerance* would be remade with a new modern story. But, a few years later, the plan was only that *One Exciting Night* would be remade inexpensively with the original climactic footage of the hurricane reused in the new version.

In 1933, Griffith did a series of radio shows for the Mutual Network and Ponds cosmetics, presenting a somewhat romanticized version of his own life and the early days of the movies. These broadcasts emanated from Hollywood, and Griffith returned there and sold his interest in United Artists for $300,000. Perhaps without quite realizing it, he thereby shut off his only route for a return to films. Griffith began protesting that he was simply enjoying life for the first time, that he wasn't working because he wanted to get off the Hollywood merry-go-round and indulge himself in the pleasures he had never had time for before. Some people believed him.

When the newly formed Museum of Modern Art in New York approached him on behalf of its film library, he pretended to be somewhat bemused that anyone would be interested in his old pictures. He assumed rather the same attitude he had taken at Biograph toward those "opiates for the masses," as he called them, borrowing Karl Marx's defamation of religion.

Griffith was not exactly poor. He had some investments and some royalties. He sold a large house he had owned, and money just seemed to turn up now and then. A New Orleans bank was being rebuilt and a safe-deposit box in Griffith's name was discovered with $100,000 in cash. The old Alexandria Hotel in Hollywood, where he had stopped in his early days, had been torn down and among its effects was an envelope with Griffith's name on it that contained $20,000 in bills. But, as Lillian Gish remarked, Griffith never knew what to do with money unless he could use it to make a film.

Griffith moved back to Kentucky in late 1933. He said that he was going to live at La Grange on the farm of his brother Will, but he soon moved into the Brown Hotel in Louisville and became a fixture in the bar, the Bluegrass Room. Days became months. Griffith could be seen, nattily dressed, brooding in the Bluegrass Room; or in the lobby of the Brown; or strolling along the Louisville streets. In his room, he worked intermittently on an autobiography which he called *D. W. and the Wolf* (the wolf was poverty at the door), and on a history of mankind which he cynically titled *The Treadmill*. And so he lived for several years.

Griffith and Linda Arvidson had never secured a divorce. She had been constantly after him for support money, and he had frequently been remiss in sending it. Now he did get a divorce, and, in March of 1936, he suddenly and unexpectedly married a young woman named Evelyn Baldwin. She was 27, and Griffith, at 61, was as ardent as an 18-year-old. He had known Miss Baldwin and her mother for some years. They met at a benefit at the Hotel Astor in New York when Evelyn was only 13. Immediately, he expressed a desire to cast the young lady as Little Nell in a production of Dickens's *Old Curiosity Shop* and even tested her for the role. Later, he renewed his acquaintance with the Baldwins and used Evelyn in a small role in *The Struggle*. For her part, she apparently cared little for a film career and was at first confused by the whole experience. During the honeymoon, the couple visited Hollywood, where Griffith joined his old friend W. S. Van Dyke on the set of *San Francisco,* a film which at its climax re-created the 1906 earthquake. "Just for fun," as he put it, Griffith took over direction of one of the final crowd scenes. The Griffiths were soon back at the Brown Hotel in Louisville. On Kentucky Derby Day, at Churchill Downs, they appeared in a purple Mercedes, with Griffith in a grey suit with matching purple tie and hat. Otherwise, D. W. resumed his vigils in the lobby and his walks along the streets.

Three years passed. Then quite suddenly Griffith was a transformed man. The glum, tried look was gone. His face was flushed and smiling, his carriage jaunty. He was returning to Hollywood to work as advisor—*director,* according to some announcements—on a film to be called *One Million B.C.* for producer Hal Roach. He was also taking to Hollywood as the film's star a handsome young man named Victor Mature, who had been working as a candy salesman. The story of just what happened during work on *One Million B.C.* is clouded by conflicting reports and opinions. The film had to do with primitive man, caveman, and it anachronistically mixed in dinosaurs (actually they were lizards with added fins and make-up, photographed on miniature sets) and wooly mammoths (actually elephants with make-up). And the film's plotlines rather resembled Griffith's Biographs *Man's Genesis* and *In Prehistoric Days*.

Hal Roach has said Griffith's advice was always helpful and the relationship between them was good. Lillian Gish reports Griffith "simply could not work in harness," and, when a difference arose,

Griffith was likely to order the producer off his own set. When *One Million B.C.* was released, Griffith's name was no longer on it. But there are some shots and images in the finished film that might be worthy of him. Griffith wrote to a friend at the time that the experience had taught him something. He felt that film had fully survived the impact of sound, and he had rediscovered that the basic silent techniques were still valid. The best directors—he named Frank Capra and Lewis Milestone—had simply heightened silent technique with sound.

Griffith stayed on in Hollywood. There were some offers of friendship, and even of work, but increasingly Griffith—his pride as vulnerable as ever and suspecting their motives were charitable rather than complimentary—found it difficult to accept them, and, increasingly, he abused his friends. The director George Cukor wanted Metro-Goldwyn-Mayer to pension Griffith for his contribution to films. The industry, after all, had pensioned Max Reinhardt whose chief contribution had been to the stage. Louis B. Mayer, who had built M.G.M., told Griffith how he had got his start by buying up the New England "states' rights" to *The Birth of a Nation* after it had played in the major cities, and how he had gone deeply into debt to do it, selling and mortgaging everything he had—even pawning his wife's jewelry. But that was the end of it; there was no pension. There were tributes, to be sure. He was given an honorary doctorate of literature by the University of Louisville. He was given an "Oscar" by the Academy of Motion Picture Arts and Sciences. He was given honorary membership in the Screen Directors Guild. But there was no work, and, as one observer put it, "What does a man full of vitality care for the honors of the past?"

There is no simple accounting for the character of so complex a man as D. W. Griffith. Similarly, there is no simple accounting for the nature of his talent, or for his decline after 1924. But without suggesting that we have arrived at a full explanation, perhaps some of the things that have been said about his later years can be pulled together. We have noted that, although Griffith said he set up at

Mamaroneck to free himself of studio pressures, some people felt that he had so isolated himself that he was far out of touch with the world around him. Herb Sterne was more specific in his remark that Griffith had "made the virginal the vogue" and that, when the vogue in feminine types changed in the 1920s, he lost his audience. Perhaps Sterne put the matter the wrong way around. Perhaps the virginal was at first simply there in the collective sensibility, in the *zeitgeist,* waiting to be expressed on film. And Griffith the artist was in touch with it. In her autobiography, Coleen Moore—an actress popular in the late 1920s for her portrayal of flapper types—declared that "Griffith loved Carol Dempster and lost his money and creativity trying to make a star out of that non-actress." Others have agreed. There is a later event that also sheds light. In 1935, Griffith went to England. The proposal was that he should direct a remake of *Broken Blossoms.* When he was having script and cast difficulties with his producers, Twickenham Films, in his desperation, Griffith telephoned Lillian Gish in New York. "Lillian! Lillian!," he pleaded. "Why did you leave me? Why aren't you here? Nobody can do this except you."

When Griffith was first attracted to Evelyn Baldwin, it was because of her small-boned face and body, her blonde curls. She *was,* he told her, Dickens's Little Nell. D. W. Griffith was indeed possessed by an image of the female innocent. She was a main subject of his films. She was also his muse. She was the guardian of his inner being. She was his Beatrice who guided his sensibilities through the world of artistic images. She was the focal point through which he saw human existence and human aspirations, through which he assessed human virtue and human vice.

Mary Pickford could carry that image and portray it for him in the early days of Biograph. Indeed, it may have been she, after Dickens's works, who first awakened the image in him. But there was an element of implicit shrewdness in Miss Pickford's portrayals that did not quite fit Griffith's inner vision. He sensed it, perhaps, and that is why he argued and fought with her as he did with few other actresses or actors. Mae Marsh could carry and portray Griffith's vision. But even in her teens Mae Marsh's presence subtly suggested the matronly woman she would become with the years. Lillian Gish could portray Griffith's inner vision—sublimely so. While he was working with these actresses, Griffith's image of woman was in touch with the times, with late Victorian feelings in the public mind and abroad in the land, about woman and about the world. By using Carol Dempster as his star, however, Griffith created a two-fold problem. Griffith was imposing his vision on a woman it did not really fit, a woman who (despite the effective performance he got out of her in *The Sorrows of Satan*) was not really an actress. At the same time, the popular image of woman was changing—another, more aggressive aspect of the feminine began to have meaning for the public. Griffith was left with a vision that fewer and fewer people found meaningful, and with no one to convey that vision for him.

Similar things have happened to other important directors. When Joseph Von Sternberg found Marlene Dietrich in Berlin where he was directing *The Blue Angel,* he found—perhaps he created—an actress who could carry an image of the cynical *femme fatale* that was deeply meaningful to himself and to many in his audience, and he directed Miss Dietrich through a series of celebrated films. But when they separated—she eventually to undertake, in *Destry Rides Again,* a sly, humorous version, even a parody, of her former screen character—Sternberg's career at last foundered. Likewise, when the Swedish director Mauritz Stiller, who discovered Greta Garbo, was brought to Hollywood, he insisted that she be brought, too, but there they were separated by studio heads. She was able to portray a worldly-wise and tragic version of the *femme fatale* for a number of directors for over ten years. Stiller directed some American films, but he soon returned to Sweden, and there he simply withered and died—as though his soul had been taken away from him.

By 1947, it was evident that D. W. Griffith's second marriage had failed. His drinking had become quite heavy and "cures" in several sanitariums did not seem to help. Finally, Evelyn Baldwin asked for a divorce and Griffith, admitting that he was "a bachelor at heart," did not contest it. Griffith stayed on in Hollywood like a tragic ghost haunting the place. He no longer had the strength even to beat at the doors that were barred to him. He moved into the small Knickerbocker Hotel, and stayed in his room by day, taking no telephone calls and ignoring his mail. By night, he roamed the streets and visited the bars, unrecognized.

One morning in late July of 1948, he was suddenly hit with a cerebral hemorrhage. He somehow stumbled into the lobby of the Knickerbocker and collapsed. The hotel physician was summoned and Griffith was taken to Temple Hospital, where he died the following morning, July 23, 1948, without having regained consciousness. When Mae Marsh visited the funeral parlor where his body lay in state, it was in the company of the great director John Ford. An attendant revealed that only four other people had visited. One of them was Cecil B. De Mille. At his funeral in Hollywood (before a final burial at Crestwood) Griffith's lifelong friend Herb Sterne refused to sit with the other honorary pallbearers because some of them—producers and others—were men who could have given Griffith help and work, but had not.

Donald Crisp, then acting president of the Academy of Motion Picture Arts and Sciences, spoke one of two eulogies and said, in part, "Difficult as it may have been for him to have played a subordinate role, I do not believe that the fault was entirely his own. I cannot help feeling that there should always have been a place for him and his talent in the motion-picture field. It is hard to believe that the industry could not have found use for his great gift." It was too late for anyone to act on Crisp's words. As Lionel Barrymore wrote in the August 1948 issue of the magazine *The Screen Writer,* "D. W. Griffith is dead and there is wailing and gnashing of teeth. Yes, but a trifle belatedly." The same actor-director said in his autobiography, *We Barrymores,* "It is an abiding mystery and scandal to me that an ungrateful industry has not raised a statue to him ninety feet tall at the intersection of Hollywood Boulevard and Vine Street. The statue should be of solid gold." There is no statue of Griffith in Hollywood, not ninety nor even six feet tall, and not of gold nor even of bronze. There is not even a plaque.

Bibliography

Agee, James, *Agee on Film,* McDowell, Obolensky Inc., New York, 1958.

Barry, Iris, *D. W. Griffith, American Film Master,* with an annotated list of films by Eileen Bowser, Museum of Modern Art, New York, 1965.

Bitzer, G. W., *Billy Bitzer: His Story,* Farrar, Straus & Giroux, New York, 1973.

Brown, Karl, *Adventures with D. W. Griffith,* Farrar, Straus & Giroux, New York, 1973.

Brownlow, Kevin, *The Parade's Gone By . . . ,* Alfred A. Knopf, Inc., New York, 1968.

Cooper, Miriam, *Dark Lady of the Silents,* Bobbs-Merrill Co., New York, 1973.

Croce, Arlene, "D. W. G. Returns," in *Rally!,* vol. 1, no. 1, 1966.

Everson, William K., "The Films of D. W. Griffith, 1907-1939," *Screen Facts* magazine, vol. 1, no. 3, May-June, 1963.

Everson, William K., *American Silent Film,* Oxford University Press, New York, 1978.

Fenin, George N. and William K. Everson, "David W. Griffith and Thomas H. Ince: 1909-1913," in *The Western,* The Orion Press, New York, 1962, pp. 60-72.

Gish, Lillian, with Ann Pinchot, *The Movies, Mr. Griffith, and Me,* Prentice-Hall, Englewood Cliffs, N.J., 1969.

Griffith, Mrs. D. W., *When the Movies Were Young*, E. P. Dutton & Co., New York, 1925.

Hart, James (ed.), *The Man Who Invented Hollywood: The Autobiography of D. W. Griffith: A Memoir and Some Notes*, Touchstone Publishing, New York, 1972.

Henderson, Robert M., *D. W. Griffith: The Years at Biograph*, Farrar, Straus & Giroux, New York, 1970.

Henderson, Robert M., *D. W. Griffith: His Life and Work*, Oxford University Press, New York, 1972.

Huff, Theodore, *Intolerance: The Film by David Wark Griffith, Shot-by-Shot Analysis*, The Museum of Modern Art, New York, 1966.

Jacobs, Lewis, *The Rise of the American Film, A Critical History* with an essay: *Experimental Cinema in America—1921-1947*, Teachers College Press, New York, 1968.

Kerr, Walter, *The Silent Clowns*, Alfred Knopf, New York, 1975.

Macgowan, Kenneth, *Behind the Screen*, Dell Publishing Co., Inc., New York, 1965.

Niver, Kemp R., *D. W. Griffith's The Battle at Elderbush Gulch*, Locare Research Group, Los Angeles, 1972.

Niver, Kemp R., *D. W. Griffith: His Biograph Films in Perspective*, Historical Films, Los Angeles, 1974.

Ramsaye, Terry, *A Million and One Nights*, Simon and Schuster, New York, 1964.

Slide, Antony, *The Griffith Actresses*, A. S. Barnes, New York, 1970.

Slide, Antony, *Early American Cinema*, A. S. Barnes, New York, 1970.

Stern, Seymour, "Griffith: I—'The Birth of a Nation,'" *Film Culture*, No. 36, Spring-Summer, 1965.

Wagenknecht, Edward and Antony Slide, *The Films of D. W. Griffith*, Crown Publishers, New York, 1975.

Note: The career and historical articles and the letters columns in the magazine *Films in Review* offer valuable research material on film history. I have made particular use of the following:

Seymour Stern's articles on early films and Griffith (the issues of Nov. 1951, Oct. 1952, and Feb. and May 1956)

George Geltzer on Rex Ingram (May 1952)

Jean R. Debrix on "Film Editing" (Jan. 1953)

Gerald D. McDonald on the "Origin of the Star System" (Nov. 1953)

Robert Downing on Lionel Barrymore (Jan. 1955)

William K. Everson on Eric Von Stroheim (Aug.-Sept. 1957)

Jack Jacobs on Richard Barthelmess (Jan. 1958)

Harold Dunham on Mae Marsh (June-July 1958)

Harold Dunham on Bessie Love (Feb. 1959)

Lucy Tupper on "Dickens on the Screen" (March 1959)

Romono Tozzi on Lillian Gish (Dec. 1962)

Harold Dunham on Bobby Harron (Dec. 1963)

Jack Spears on "Mary Pickford's Directors" (Feb. 1966)

DeWitt Bodeen on Wallace Reid (April 1966)

Jack Spears on Norma Talmadge (Jan. 1967)

DeWitt Bodeen on Constance Talmadge (Dec. 1967)

DeWitt Bodeen on Dorothy Gish (Aug.-Sept. 1968)

Robert Giroux on Mack Sennett (Dec. 1968 and Jan. 1969)

Jack Spears on Edwin S. Porter (June-July 1970)

Clayton M. Steinman's article, "Shadow in the Cave: D. W. Griffith and 'One Million B.C.'" (Jan. 1976)

Alfonso Pinto on Lupe Velez (Nov. 1977)

DeWitt Bodeen on "Joseph Hergesheimer and Films" (Nov. 1977)

And *Films in Review* for October 1975 was a Griffith Centennial issue, with articles by Wagenknecht, Slide, Everson, Bitzer, and others.

Index